Praise for *The Final*

"In this remarkable, potent, and deeply origir
Gaspard gives us ways to explore and inhabit the gift of safely and
creatively living with personas beyond the local ego. What becomes
possible then is an emergent humanity that is equal to the challenges of our time."

— **Jean Houston,** PhD, author of *The Possible Human* and
chancellor of Meridian University

"This exuberant book introduces us to the rich diversity of our inner
selves. At the same time deep and lighthearted, *The Final 8th* is the
perfect guidebook for breaking through impasses that stand —
unconsciously — in the way of our fullest development and the
achievement of our desired goals."

— **Peeka Trenkle,** MDiv, founder of the Green Medicine program
at the New York Open Center

"An engagingly written, candid, and very useful guide for those who
are stuck and don't know why. I plan to steal many of Bridgit's ideas!"

— **Phillip Lopate,** author of *Portrait Inside My Head*

"*The Final 8th* is a recipe for true embodied success. Bridgit is a master of transforming wounds into superpowers. She will guide you to
achieve your dream and become more whole in the process."

— **Ruthie Fraser,** author of *Stack Your Bones*

"Using the voice dialogue process to break through persistent personal blocks is a brilliant innovation. But it's not something to try
on one's own. To succeed requires unparalleled support and guidance. Luckily, that's exactly what Bridgit provides in this book. Follow her lead, and the magic will surely unfold."

— **Raphael Cushnir,** author of *The One Thing Holding You Back*

"As an integrative health expert, I am always on the lookout for resources to help my clients through their stuckness. In this vibrant
era of hooking into your potential, Bridgit introduces a potent

technique called voice dialogue. Her book will walk you through how to unlock your intentions, dismantle your conflicting loyalties, and solve the mystery of your self-sabotage. You will find your journey through Bridgit's book both energizing and transformational."

— **Alena Gerst,** LCSW, RYT, author of
A Wellness Handbook for the Performing Artist

"*The Final 8th* makes overcoming roadblocks, limiting beliefs, or resistance to finishing any project a creative process of self-discovery. I love Bridgit's tender, humorous, and light touch in making some of our greatest challengers into our lifelong friends. And with this tool bag filled with tools, our obstacles transform into stepping-stones on each of our unique paths. This book is a gift."

— **J. Tamar Stone,** senior voice dialogue facilitator

"Having taught thousands of people the art of creative vision, I have come to understand that you can do 'all the right things' and still struggle with accomplishing your goal. Bridgit unravels the mystery of why you are stuck in a simple, easy-to-understand way. The final eighth process liberates you to truly go from impasse to kickass."

— **Barbara Biziou,** vision coach and author of *The Joy of Ritual*

"*The Final 8th* is profoundly transformational. It's also wise, warm, and very accessible. Bridgit Dengel Gaspard is masterful at breaking down a critical self-growth process that is sure to change your life. Read this brilliant book to become whole, and also free."

— **Laura Zam,** certified trauma professional and author of
The Pleasure Plan: One Woman's Search for Sexual Healing

"Stuckness can be paralyzing, and that's when you need help. I highly recommend *The Final 8th*, which gives you a wildly new type of GPS to access the parts of yourself you've lost, like your creative, curious, and optimistic alter egos."

— **J. Plunky Branch,** founder of N.A.M.E. Brand Records
and Plunky & Oneness

"Bridgit Dengel Gaspard has written an important and amazing book about working with and healing our inner conflicts. To this end, she has brought the voice dialogue method to the world in a way that is profoundly accessible and strikingly contemporary. Here we learn that we have many parts or selves within us and that they do not all want the same things. She shows us how to use voice dialogue and other strategies to bring these parts out into the open so that healing and resolution may occur. Filled with evocative and compelling examples, *The Final 8th* gives us a way to use all our inner resources and to dramatically improve our lives. This book is a gift."

— **Scott Kellogg, PhD,** director of the Transformational
Chairwork Psychotherapy Project, New York City

"*The Final 8th* provides readers with an invaluable voice dialogue approach to understanding their unique stuckness, but those who read *and engage with* the book's abundant, accessible, and clear exercises will shift their relationships with and resolve, often in unexpected ways, those pesky last steps toward their goals. Bridgit Dengel Gaspard, through her deep life experience, clarity of thought, ability to surprise, and playful wit, comes alive and becomes a trustworthy ally on these pages."

— **Reggie Marra,** author of *Killing America,*
The Quality of Effort, and *And Now, Still*

"As a leadership and relationship coach who has been on a personal growth path for thirty years, I've had my share of struggles with failure. I love that this book gave me a fresh and innovative way of dealing with the parts of me who want to live life fully, and other parts who totally want to sabotage me. Who knew? I only wish I'd read this twenty years ago! The exercises in this book are life changing, with humor and fun to spice it up. A solid-gold-10-must-read for anyone who wants to make a bigger impact on the planet!"

— **Jeannie Daly-Gunter, MA,** cofounder of the Transformative
Loving Institute and author of *The Love Map:*
Reignite, Reconnect, and Repair Your Relationship

"In this warm, wise, and witty book, Bridgit Dengel Gaspard unlocks the mystery of why we don't complete our passion projects. Her insights into this phenomenon are original and hugely practical and helpful. If you want to go for your dreams but don't know why you feel stuck, this is the book for you. A real eye-opener."

— **Brian Tom O'Connor,** author of *Awareness Games: Playing with Your Mind to Create Joy* and cohost of the podcast *Awareness Explorers*

"Having experienced Bridgit's work in person numerous times, I am elated to see her magic now available in this wonderful book. *The Final 8th* adds fresh new insights to help you go all the way with your goal. In the process you transform from being a contender to being victorious."

— **Brett Bevell,** Omega program strategist, faculty, and author

"Bridgit offers a brilliant, innovative, and compassionate approach to problem solving. Once she articulated the concept of the final eighth and spelled out the steps required for authentic and meaningful success, I thought, 'Of course! This makes perfect sense!' But I wouldn't have thought of them without her wonderful, workable process."

— **Fran Sorin,** author of *Digging Deep: Unearthing Your Creative Roots through Gardening*

"This book is a master class in understanding your inner voice by embracing your final eighth and reaching your greatest potential. Each chapter guides you to learn, listen, and transform your inner self and embark on life's greatest rewards."

— **Joe Taravella, PhD,** licensed clinical psychologist

"If you have an unfinished novel in a drawer, perfect gym attendance for the first two weeks of January and not the rest of the year, or any number of incomplete projects weighing you down, this book is for you. This is a dynamic guide to crossing the finish line — whatever your goal may be. Bridgit Dengel Gaspard offers concrete, insightful techniques that will have you breaking through your personal barriers to achieve your desires. Give yourself the gift of accomplishment with this fun and fast read."

— **Beth Stevens,** Emmy-winning writer and managing editor of broadway.com

the
final 8th

the
final

8th

Enlist Your Inner Selves
to Accomplish Your Goals

Bridgit Dengel Gaspard

Foreword by Hal and Sidra Stone

New World Library
Novato, California

New World Library
14 Pamaron Way
Novato, California 94949

Text design by Tona Pearce Myers

Library of Congress Cataloging-in-Publication Data

Names: Gaspard, Bridgit Dengel, date, author.
Title: The final 8th : enlist your inner selves to accomplish your goals / Bridgit Dengel Gaspard.
Other titles: Final eighth
Description: Novato, California : New World Library, [2020] | Includes bibliographical references and index. | Summary: "A psychologist discusses the phenomenon of talented and ambitious people stalling at "the final eighth" on the way to a cherished goal, often because of self-defeating behaviors. The author proposes a therapeutic method known as "Inner Voice Dialogue" to help readers resolve inner conflicts and achieve ultimate success."-- Provided by publisher.
Identifiers: LCCN 2020007025 (print) | LCCN 2020007026 (ebook) |
    ISBN 9781608686919 (paperback ; alk. paper) | ISBN 9781608686926 (epub)
Subjects: LCSH: Goal (Psychology) | Self-talk. | Motivation (Psychology)
    | Self-defeating behavior.
Classification: LCC BF505.G6 G37 2020 (print) | LCC BF505.G6 (ebook) |
    DDC 153.8/5--dc23
LC record available at https://lccn.loc.gov/2020007025
LC ebook record available at https://lccn.loc.gov/2020007026

First printing, July 2020
ISBN 978-1-60868-691-9
Ebook ISBN 978-1-60868-692-6
Printed in the US on 30% postconsumer-waste recycled paper

New World Library is proud to be a Gold Certified Environmentally Responsible Publisher. Publisher certification awarded by Green Press Initiative.

10   9   8   7   6   5   4   3   2   1

To my beloved husband and partner in life,
Ray Gaspard, who definitely prefers some of my selves
over others, but honors each one

Contents

Foreword

We must admit that — in keeping with the title of this delightfully entertaining and extremely helpful book — we have been stuck in our own "final eighth." Somehow it took us *forever* to find the time to write this foreword! Why might that be?

We are both curious creatures, and our lives have been dedicated to the exploration of the human psyche, with all its complexity and contradictions. Consciousness in its many forms has always fascinated us. So this "stuckness" that Bridgit Dengel Gaspard addresses in her book gave us something new to consider.

As we pondered this matter, we realized that we may well have reached the "final eighth" of our lives. We are currently eighty-two and ninety-one years old, and our explorations are taking us in new directions. But, even as there was much for us to discover when we were first together almost fifty years ago, there remain fascinating new discoveries to be made now.

The tools of voice dialogue that we developed in the 1970s and the maps of the archetypal bonding patterns in the interactions of these multiple inner selves that helped us to navigate past decades continue to be helpful in this new and unfamiliar territory. And as Bridgit points out, this final eighth brings up the need to separate yet again from our primary selves (the ones that have given us such rich and exciting lives), to feel the vulnerability of reaching the end of our lives, and to explore and nurture the selves that will be the greatest help in creatively and successfully navigating this next part of life's journey.

Bridgit's unique concept of the final eighth, and this guidebook for navigating through the often difficult terrain of completion, embraces a practical and concrete way of using our work. With memorable anecdotes that illustrate her pragmatic approach to this challenge, she helps you to carefully examine your desire to cross the finish line, to discover what is holding you back from doing so, and to have greater conscious choice as you take the steps necessary to move ahead. With thought-provoking exercises and practical suggestions, she invites you on fascinating and rewarding explorations of your many selves as she supports you in the completion of your own final eighth.

We're certain that you will enjoy this remarkable journey.

DRS. HAL AND SIDRA STONE
Creators of Voice Dialogue
Authors of *Embracing Our Selves: The Voice Dialogue Manual*

Introduction

Failing within Sight of Victory

Everybody dies, but not everybody lives.

— DRAKE, in Nicki Minaj's "Moment 4 Life"

*Meet your inner selves and discover their secret
and powerful intentions and distorted loyalties that
are locking you into a double bind.*

It's painful to find yourself seriously stuck. Despite doing all
the right things, inexplicably you're unable to reach a long-
held goal, whether it's in your career, your relationships, your
finances, your creative life, your health, or your personal growth.
Most of us endure a bout of paralysis at some point in our lives.
It happens to CEOs and moms and CEOs who are moms; to students and teachers; to doctors and dancers; and to young adults,
techies, and retirees. But being stuck when you are so close to

success is a distinct phenomenon. It feels even worse when you are in sight of the finish line, yet you don't cross it.

I've worked with many clients — talented, energetic, motivated women and men — who had accomplished multiple steps toward their goal but were unable to complete it. These are driven, enterprising folks who are doers — and who were highly dissatisfied with their situation but unable to change it. They found themselves immobilized on the way to a cherished aspiration, from choosing a career to finding a mate, from getting out of debt to building a boat, from loving themselves to becoming a master plumber. I began to call this treacherous, demoralizing quandary the final eighth (and to refer to everything going before it as the first seven-eighths).

We all have a challenge we want to push through. The final eighth process is a breakthrough metaphor, a fresh new paradigm for the process of taking the steps necessary to complete a project, finish a goal, realize a dream, and flourish.

What follows are final eighth scenarios my clients have experienced. Some may strike a chord with you.

I've tried online dating, I've told everyone I know that I'm looking, I've gone to singles events, and I've kissed a lot of frogs, but I just can't find mate material — it feels hopeless.

I've got a great idea for a small business. I've done the research, and I've lined up potential investors who are ready with the seed money. They're just waiting for my business plan, but I can't seem to draft it — I feel stupid.

I visited colleges and picked my top five. I can't wait to graduate. I filled out applications, but when it comes to writing my personal essay, I freeze up — I feel I don't have anything important to say.

I decided I wanted to make peace with my dad. We've always had a difficult relationship. I went to therapy, I've talked things over with my siblings and my husband, I've practiced what I want to say. I feel so ready, but I just can't make the call — I feel powerless.

I've saved enough money for a down payment, my credit history is great, and having my own home is something I've always wanted, but for some reason I stop myself every time I'm about to make an offer — I get so angry at myself.

Do any of these stories sound familiar? You have your act together, you seem to be in high gear, you're doing everything you can consciously think of to reach your goal, you're getting good feedback — and yet you wind up stalling and feeling bad.

Understanding the concept of the final eighth can help you escape that bind, cross that finish line, and not only revel in the sweet smell of success, but also learn how to extend your championship season by practicing *safe* success.

The First Seven-Eighths

When you're stuck in the final stages of achieving a goal, whether it is to become solvent, get a dog, or gain a promotion, you've probably done everything pretty much right. You took the initiative, followed a plan, and moved toward your goal. This is the first seven-eighths. It includes successes, failures, and procrastinations — in other words, all the different experiences that have led to your current level of wisdom.

The first seven-eighths can include the following:

- grappling with challenging habits but having difficulty finding support
- discovering your passion but not knowing how to empower it
- gaining physical strength but not being able to maintain progress
- boosting your emotional health but losing it under stress
- getting experience in your profession but not being able to move up
- studying but struggling with completing courses for credit

When the finish line is within sight, shimmering with promise, you just can't get there. Despite the nearness to the goal, despite your hard work, despite the access to necessary resources, despite your admirable level of commitment, you find yourself unable to take the final steps to success. And sadly, you may have been in this position more than once.

My clients were baffled about why they were stuck. They reported feeling frustrated, stressed, sad, and scared. "I just don't get it," they'd say. "I'm doing everything I can think of. This is what I want more than anything, and I just can't take the next step. Why is this happening?" They'd swear to me they yearned for the desired outcome with every fiber of their being.

I'd tell them, "Believe it or not, some of those fibers just aren't with the program." The truth is, *not every part of you wants what you think you want!* Some of your inner selves are opposed to your goal. We'll explore the technique of voice dialogue, a powerful method developed by my mentors, Hal and Sidra Stone, to discover those different aspects of yourself and speak from their point of view. This technique can reveal and free you from the hidden internal conflict that's blocking your ability to achieve your goal.

In addition, you'll discover other parts of yourself: a secret team of wise counselors, canny advisers, and magical sages who can give you just the guidance you need, to shift your perspective, reveal your buried strengths, and get you rolling again toward success and fulfillment. They are within you! I explain exactly how anyone can contact these inner guides, also called *selves, subpersonalities, alter egos,* and *personas,* who will help you in the art of finishing. Through an innovative series of self-guided exercises, you'll discover and communicate with these creative, resourceful, opinionated parts of yourself and tap into their strengths in order to cross the finish line. My approach energizes and liberates people anywhere on the stuckness spectrum, regardless of the specific issue, because the difficulties spring from similar headwaters.

How This Book Works

I recognized the final eighth phenomenon because once upon a time (by which I mean for decades) I lived it. The final eighth process combines my personal, creative, and clinical experience with new and proven techniques for self-discovery and problem solving. Each chapter of this book builds on the next. After you identify your final eighth project, you explore your inner world to discover what's getting in the way of completion. As you gain insights and inspirations, you can take concrete action toward your goal.

You will find out how to identify and speak with your inner selves to uncover their secret intentions and figure out which of them support your goal and which are impeding it. You will learn to spot and discard the negative beliefs — painful disinformation such as "I'm worthless" or "I'm stupid" — that are holding you back. You will discover which personas are clinging to these beliefs and imprisoning you. Gaining this knowledge, resolving the dilemma within, and discovering your creative, brave, resourceful team of inner selves boosts the vitality you need to fulfill your cherished goal and cross the finish line.

Support from Brain Research
for the Final Eighth Process

Inner dialogue has an enormous effect on individuals' success in life. Recent investigations in neuroscience are confirming observations by pioneer therapists like Hal and Sidra Stone. As the Yale psychology professor Paul Bloom wrote in the *Atlantic*, "Many researchers now believe, to varying degrees, that each of us is a community of competing selves.... Considerable evidence, including recent brain-imaging studies, suggests... that the selves have different memories and personalities."

The way we access and communicate with these inner selves can powerfully affect our decisions and actions. *Psychology Today* profiled the research of Dr. Ethan Kross, director of the Emotion and Self-Control Laboratory at the University of Michigan, examining the power of our natural impulse to refer to ourselves in the third person, especially in stressful situations. In a series of groundbreaking experiments, Kross found that "by toggling the way we address the self — first person or third — we flip a switch in the cerebral cortex, the center of thought, and another in the amygdala, the seat of fear, moving closer to or further from our sense of self and all its emotional intensity."

The concept of inner selves has nothing to do with multiple personalities, the condition now called dissociative identity disorder. Forget *Sibyl*, forget *The Three Faces of Eve*. A long and distinguished line of theorists and practitioners have acknowledged the idea of a *healthy* personality consisting of many subpersonalities and have embraced the discipline called parts therapy. They include Sigmund Freud, Carl Jung, Roberto Assagioli, Fritz Perls, Eric Berne, Virginia Satir, Nathaniel Branden, Hal and Sidra Stone, Lucia Capacchione, Richard Schwartz, Todd Herman, and many others.

The Process

Chapter 1 gives an overview of the final eighth process. In chapter 2, you learn how inner selves form, and you identify the circumstances that determined which personas you lead with and which ones you hide. Chapter 3 presents detailed instructions for communicating with your primary selves, the ones you know best, using voice dialogue to gather wisdom from each self. In chapter 4, you discover the hidden selves who are stopping you from achieving your goals, the subpersonalities that you'd like to hide or wish away — and some you may not have met yet. Chapter 5 shows you how to communicate directly with these hidden selves and learn the reasons behind your mysterious inability to finish your project.

In chapter 6, you identify the false negative beliefs that are keeping you from succeeding. You'll look closely at the rules derived from these beliefs, which dictate how you live: what you expect from yourself and others, what you're entitled to, and what's forbidden (like success). In chapter 7 we expose the invisible and unresolvable dilemma called a double bind, created by the contradiction between your goals and your core negative beliefs. Identifying and releasing your double bind is a unique and crucial component of the final eighth process.

Chapter 8 invites you to consider abandoning your final eighth goal. (Yes, really!) But if you decide to stick with it, your journey will now include practicing safe success.

Chapter 9 addresses the question, "Who needs failure?" Surprisingly, many people have a negative relationship with their superpowers. This chapter explores the possibility that you may be ceding control of your life to substances and to fantasies like the mirage goal, which you continue to pursue but never achieve. It presents unique methods to detoxify the parts of yourself that are still devoted to *not* succeeding and an effective tool for handling pitfalls like envy. In chapter 10, you decide whether some of your inner selves, including your Inner Critic, are performing outdated roles and learn how to assign them new roles. You also identify and enlist the help of powerful, potent parts of yourself that are vital to completing your final eighth goal. In chapter 11, it's time to celebrate your crossing your finish line and completing your final eighth goal.

In chapter 12, you apply safe-success guidelines to help you adjust happily to the often disorienting reality of achieving your dream. Now that you can spot which inner selves are active at any given moment, you can deal with potential self-sabotage by making conscious choices about which personas lead you.

All the exercises and activities in this book have been road tested by me and my clients, students, and workshop participants and declared doable and useful. (In examples that describe my clients' experiences, identifying details such as names and specific circumstances have been changed to protect privacy.) Sometimes people feel uncomfortable when they first try identifying inner selves and then speaking as those subpersonalities. But they soon become accustomed to the voice dialogue process and acknowledge its value.

Perhaps your I-Need-a-Guarantee self wants to know if the final eighth process always works. I can say that even the skittish, the skeptics, and the stonewallers I've encountered have benefited from the insights and exercises in this book.

One workshop participant who'd been stuck professionally for a long time jumped into the voice dialogue process and soon afterward found herself having to choose between two career-boosting job offers. She marveled, "What? Do your dreams just start coming true when you start doing voice dialogue?"

I can't explain it, but I've seen it happen. A lot. The final eighth process frees you by helping you access your wonderful team of inner selves, developing courage, strength, and creativity, and accessing the resources you need to break through your impasse and reach your goal.

Militant Self-Care

Some of the self-exploration and exercises in this book can be mentally and emotionally challenging. If you get to the point where you're thinking, "I just don't want to deal with any of this right now!," stop the exercise and instead practice what I like to call militant self-care.

This is any activity that nurtures your mental, emotional, and physical health. Self-care improves your mood and reduces your anxiety by boosting positive feelings, confidence, and self-esteem. Self-care cushions us against criticism and negativity from the world, helping us stand up to threats and persevere in difficult situations.

Self-care even makes you smarter! The psychologists Clayton Critcher and David Dunning of the University of California at Berkeley researched the effects of giving yourself feel-good ego boosts like positive affirmations and found they broaden your mindset. Self-care widens our perspective on all of our selves, alleviating defensiveness and expanding our view. And that's what the final eighth process does too! Do you prefer a state of constriction or a state of expansion? (There's really only one right answer.)

Self-care can consist simply of doing something you truly enjoy — something that makes you feel comforted, protected, supported, or pampered. It could be as simple as taking a nap, playing with your dog, diving into a graphic novel, going to a movie or the driving range, baking a pie, having (ideally, amazing) sex, or gardening. Or it could be something that isn't a barrel of fun but involves actively taking care of yourself, like making a medical appointment you've been putting off, or going for a run.

I refer to this as *militant* self-care because I don't want you to let everyday chores, misplaced guilt, or even pressing job duties get in the way of your feeling better. You'll get done what needs to be done — but first, fight off the forces that are keeping you from being kind to yourself.

CHAPTER

Your Inner Selves

Not All of You Wants
What You Think You Want

I am large, I contain multitudes.

— WALT WHITMAN, "Song of Myself"

Discover your creative, brave, resourceful world of inner selves and tap into their vitality to fulfill your goal and cross the finish line.

Neal came to see me because he was stuck. An attractively bearish, informally stylish man in his thirties, Neal said he was reasonably content with work — he was the tech manager at an ad agency — and happy at home; he loved his wife and their two young daughters. But he'd set a goal he couldn't seem to reach: losing weight. Every time he came close to success, it somehow slipped away.

"I'm a man who gets things done. I find a strategy and follow through. I —"

13

He took a deep breath and blurted out, "I can't believe I'm having a problem losing my last few pounds! I thought I could handle it on my own, but my strategy has failed."

Nearly a year earlier, on their ninth wedding anniversary, Neal and his wife, Alice, had made a pact to get back to their wedding-day fitness levels by the time they celebrated their tenth, when they intended to renew their vows. They didn't do anything crazy to try to lose weight, he said; they just ate healthfully and exercised more.

"It's not that hard," he said, "I go along doing everything right, but three times now, I've been within six or seven pounds of my goal, and about to step up my workout at the gym, when something happens, and I blow it. I blow up, actually." He slumped in his chair. "Maybe you can help me come up with a game plan."

What was tripping up Neal wasn't anything that practical weight-loss tips could fix. The problem, and the solution, lay much deeper. He was being buffeted by conflicting internal forces of which he was largely unaware. No game plan in the world was going to work until he realized that even though he might swear that he yearned for the desired goal with every fiber of his being, some of those fibers — some of his inner selves — just weren't on board. *Not all of you wants what you think you want!*

Here's a simple illustration of multiple selves in action. My alarm goes off at 6 a.m. Part of me is happy that it's time to get up, get ready for the day, and meet with clients; part of me finds sleep utterly delicious and longs to stay in bed. Yet another part considers playing hooky, willing to get up only if that means spending the day alternating between beekeeping (I tend a hive in my Brooklyn backyard) and dancing. Some mornings I'm aware of a rather muted part who feels down and would prefer to spend all day alone reading and writing. A brief struggle ensues among these inner personas, so fleeting that it would barely register if I didn't already know they were there. Most mornings, my Devoted Healer and Curious-about-Life inner parts emerge — perhaps after one additional self, the Inner Negotiator, decrees that I hit the snooze button for just ten more minutes of rest. Does this sound familiar? What inner parts of you start arguing when your alarm clock rings?

Many people identify the Perfectionist, the Pleaser, and the Inner Critic among their inner selves. Others include the Rescuer, Victim, Secret Keeper, and Warrior. These selves can be aspects of the self that we describe as qualities, like *contemplative, generous, impulsive, terrified, glamorous, curious, addicted, entitled*, and *undeserving*.

After listening to Neal, I detected many possible inner selves, including Confident, Dedicated, Professional, and Polite. I asked him if he'd be willing to identify a self he'd like to communicate with using voice dialogue. "And by communicate, I don't mean role-playing or impersonating," I said. "When you embody your subpersonality, allow that inner self to be present and say what spontaneously comes up." Neal immediately named his Inner Competitor.

I had him move to another chair in the room before speaking. Neal slowly got up and after a pause, selected a nearby high-backed chair, whipped it around, straddled it, and folded his arms over the top. His energy changed entirely; his posture was upright, his body language forceful. He certainly commanded my attention.

I explained to Neal that in a voice dialogue session, when he was speaking as a subpersonality, he should use the pronoun *I* and refer to Neal in the third person. This makes it easier to hear and be open to what an alter ego has to say.

"Got it!" Neal-as-Competitor said in a commanding tone, deeper and more clipped than his earlier speech. "Neal lost most of the weight that he wants to lose, but he can't seem to drop the rest. I get him close to the goal, and then he chubs up. I get him close again, and then Neal screws things up again. I guess we're calling it a final eighth issue!"

Alice had already reached her goal, Neal-as-Competitor told me, and had maintained it for a month. "I'm really happy for her —" he said before stopping himself.

"Wait!" Neal-as-Competitor said.

"That's some other Nice-Guy-It's-All-Good part of Neal that said that. Not me!"

Gesturing toward his chest for emphasis, he went on: "For me, Neal's Competitor, Alice's loss makes me a loser! For me, life is a zero-sum game. Period. Okay, most of the time I enjoy working out....I still don't know how to pronounce *quinoa*, but bring it on! The organic stuff we eat is delicious. But then suddenly Neal is in the car eating crap from a drive-through at Burger King. It's like someone else took over the steering wheel. It's certainly not me, the Competitor. I don't really understand what happens. Neither does Neal."

When he finished speaking as the Competitor, I asked Neal to return to his original chair and sit briefly without talking, so he could feel the energy shift from the intensity of his Inner Competitor.

I congratulated him for being willing to jump so deeply

into an unfamiliar exercise. Neal smiled and said, "See? That's the advantage of having a competitive self. The rule is, if I'm going to do something, I'm going to do it well. I like the Competitor's intensity. I get things done when I'm in that energy."

I told Neal that often, being stuck or backsliding when you're close to completion is a sign that you've gone as far as you can with your current level of awareness, skills, and knowledge. Success requires new learning. I noted that in this single session he'd shown several different aspects of himself, each with something to teach him. "I saw a resourceful and a responsible alter ego that were comfortable in an unfamiliar situation," I said. "But there was also another self, one that seemed sad and found it difficult at first to reveal what you needed help with."

Neal shook his head ruefully, then nodded in agreement. "That was my Inner Loser!" he said.

"Loser, but not as in weight." He sighed. "My Competitor hates to admit that the Loser is a part of me."

Neal was quickly entering the spirit of voice dialogue. I explained that the Inner Loser is a hidden self — a part he wishes weren't there. But like it or not, there it was.

"You're aware of your Inner Loser, even though you'd prefer to ignore him. But you — like all of us — have some hidden selves you don't even know about. For example, when you were speaking as your Inner Competitor and you described Neal's ending up at the drive-through, you said it was as if someone else had taken the wheel. That someone is a hidden self, a part we definitely need to learn more about. The goal is not to eliminate any self, but to learn from it. Each self, no matter what, aims to protect your vulnerability and has a gift. We're not going to banish the Loser or any other part of you."

"Why not? I wanna banish my Loser!" Neal said, attempting a joke in a baby voice.

I explained, "Trying to get rid of an inner self doesn't work and can't be done. It's a fool's errand. Anyone who has tried to eradicate their Inner Critic knows that. What I'm helping you do is become intimate with your inner selves, so you have a direct relationship with them and stop wasting time and energy running away from parts of yourself that you don't like or that are frightening."

During our time together Neal encountered a hidden self that he had been completely unaware of — a self that was thwarting his goal for reasons that startled him. What originally appeared to be a weight problem had its roots in a different, deeper issue. Neal recognized a young, tender part of himself he called Little Louie. This alter ego was connected to an important period in Neal's childhood. Back then his only time alone with his beloved father, Louie, was on Saturdays, when the two ran errands together. They always stopped at Burger King for a cheeseburger, fries, and a milkshake. The ritual was their shared secret, since his mother would have a meal waiting when they got home.

"My dad would always say, 'I am King Louie, the King of Burgers,' and I would laugh every time. It never got old."

When Neal was twelve, his father died suddenly of a heart attack. Neal endured the loss by embracing the strong, achievement-oriented parts of himself and ignoring the hurt, vulnerable, emotional parts. His grieving mother encouraged these forceful aspects of Neal's personality. She was openly proud of his abilities, and her validation encouraged his identification with tough-guy parts of himself, to the detriment of his softer, more emotive selves.

When you ignore parts of yourself, they make themselves known indirectly. Neal eventually realized it was Little Louie who was steering him to the drive-through. Eating fast food was a way to connect with his dad by reliving their happy ritual. In our sessions, Neal allowed himself to feel his grief for his dad instead of denying it and having it burst out and sabotage his weight goal by sneaking what he jokingly came to call an "Unhappy Meal." Through the final eighth process, Neal identified his core negative belief: that he did not deserve all the happiness he now enjoyed. He came to understand that Little Louie was putting him into a double bind, making him unconsciously feel that pursuing his final eighth goal (achieving a healthy weight) was disloyal to his father.

To mark these important insights, Neal and his wife decided to honor his father by including a special mention of him when they renewed their wedding vows on their tenth anniversary. When the day came, Neal had reached his target weight; he felt sleek and grounded, and he and Alice were truly looking forward to their next ten years together.

At our final session Neal told me, "For the first time ever, I recited a poem. It was in honor of my dad, and shockingly, I wasn't nervous — I just channeled my Inner Poet! Man, when I came to see you, I really didn't know what I was getting into. Since my final eighth goal was to lose my last few pounds, I thought we'd be focusing on each and every single ounce I had to lose, and it would be boring and grueling. Instead I met my inner selves and hooked into a whole new identity."

THE FINAL EIGHTH PROCESS
Choose Your Final Eighth Goal

1. What is your final eighth goal? What task or life goal, practical or emotional, are you having trouble completing?

2. Describe the first seven-eighths in relation to that goal. What have you done already, even if it feels like nothing or a total failure? Suppose you want to ask someone out on a date, but you haven't had the nerve to actually do it. The first seven-eighths might include feeling the attraction, thinking about asking the person out, planning where you will invite them, and remembering past successful and unsuccessful dates. The first seven-eighths includes the good, the bad, and the ugly: all of it contributes to learning.

3. Describe the ideal outcome. What will completion of your final eighth goal look and feel like?

4. What do you think has kept you from reaching your final eighth goal? Write down all the reasons that come to mind: the sensible, the silly, and everything in between.

2 The Inner Selfie Report

And I am out with lanterns, looking for myself.

— EMILY DICKINSON, *The Collected Letters of Emily Dickinson*

Hard-ass truth feels like a beacon in the fog and confusion.

"My final eighth issue is, do I marry John or do we break up? I can't talk about it with my friends and family anymore, because they're sick of hearing about me and John." Sophia, a willowy fifth-grade teacher in her late twenties, was clearly miserable. This was her third attempt at a relationship with John since college. The first had lasted nine months, the second two years; they'd both dated other people while they were apart. Sophia had initiated the earlier splits.

"The first two times we were together," she said, "things started out great. But after about a year, John started driving me crazy. He's such a good guy — but he's too agreeable. I know that sounds weird, but he refuses to have an opinion about things. You know: 'Whatever you want to do; wherever you want to eat,' shrug, shrug — and I'd think, oh my God, I'm going to be stuck with this for the rest of my life! Boring! I'd turn into a raging bull, stomp around, and then snap back into myself. What's really unfair and awful is that this happened when we were really good together and John was being sweet. But that rage over nothing built up and built up until I broke things off."

Sometimes, she said, she'd look at the list of pros and cons she'd made and decide she absolutely had to break up with John. But then she'd lose her nerve, or a friend would tell her she was nuts and John was perfect for her. At other times when she looked at the list, getting married seemed like absolutely the right thing to do.

The key to Sophia's dilemma would be revealed by her inner selves. She was familiar with the idea that we're all made up of many subpersonalities, and she named some of hers.

"I've got a Pleaser, for sure," she said. "I want everyone to be happy with what I do, no matter what. The Critic is big for me too," Sophia went on. "And I have a terrified little girl in me too, yeah." She thought a minute. "My Raging Bull — is that a self?"

"Absolutely," I said. "And we'll definitely talk to it later and find out what's going on."

"We will? I'm not sure I speak bull — wait a minute, I know I do." She flashed a smile.

Where Do Inner Selves Come From?

In exploring the concept of inner selves, let's begin at the beginning. You are born completely dependent on the adults in your life to meet your physical and emotional needs. Some aspects of personality appear to be genetic: studies have shown, for example, that shyness, thrill seeking, and hyperactivity have a genetic component. But your family's responses play a huge role in determining how and whether these predispositions manifest themselves.

In babyhood, your chief task is to get your caregivers to respond to your needs, so very early on, you learn to please your caregivers as quickly and effectively as possible. From day one, your caregivers accept, reinforce, and reward some behaviors and emotional responses and discourage others through ignoring, correcting, punishing, and other signs of displeasure. To avoid their rejection, earn their approval, ensure their protection, and gain their love, you spontaneously develop the parts of yourselves to which other people respond favorably: first your parents, then extended family, babysitters, teachers, religious leaders, friends, members of your varying communities and social class, and the culture at large.

Generally, the approved parts become your primary selves — the dominant set of characteristics that you call your personality, the "you" that you talk about when you're asked to describe yourself. The disapproved parts — the ones that the important people in your lives didn't reward or value — are suppressed. But they stick around, barely acknowledged or deeply buried; these are hidden selves. Most likely you try to hide them because they make you feel embarrassed, ashamed, depressed, or anxious. They might, for instance, be the parts you consider angry, arrogant, unfocused, unfair, greedy, impatient, irresponsible, jealous, vengeful, dominating, immoral, sexual, asexual, cruel, super-sensitive, selfish, violent, drunk, or high. And even if some of these hidden selves have been stuffed away so thoroughly that you're not conscious of them, they still influence your choices and behavior — maybe even more than the acknowledged subpersonalities do.

Every single one of your inner selves, primary or hidden, has one main function: to protect your vulnerability. The classic definition of vulnerability is being open, or exposed, to attack. I characterize it as simply being open. It is the key to your unique essence, your potentiality. In childhood, your inner selves do what they can with what they have, often using blunt, primitive weapons of suppression to squelch your natural impulses and keep you safe. Sadly, this early defensive framework often creates a barrier between you and your distinctive essence. In order to protect yourself in your original environments, which is necessary for survival, you turn against vital parts of yourself, banishing them into your unconscious. Being stuck very close to achieving a goal reflects the blockade inside yourself. The final eighth process identifies and illuminates how your particular set of subpersonalities operates. You will determine which alter egos are helping you toward your goal, which ones are trapping you in a double bind, and which need retrieving.

Our inner selves are not the same as the different roles we are called upon to play in life. For our purposes, *role* refers to a social function or occupation — daughter, uncle, hostess, lawyer, cannabis barista — that any alter ego can fulfill. But different selves play these roles differently, and some are more effective than others. For example, accessing your Inner Dominator may help you win a landmark case in court, but it may not facilitate conversations with your partner or teenage son. There may be trouble at the office if your Inner Child takes over at a meeting. Our goal is to understand and have access to our inner selves so that we can choose which qualities to lead with in any given situation.

Hal and Sidra Stone, the developers of the voice dialogue method, call a baby's first primary selves the Protectors or Controllers. A Protector/Controller self is "like a bodyguard — constantly searching for dangers that may lurk around us and determining how it can best protect us from them," they write in *Embracing Our Selves*. Protector/Controller subpersonalities use this infant intelligence to begin formulating internal rules of conduct deemed appropriate for the child's particular family, and they update or solidify those rules in response to new input. This makes the world feel like a sensible, predictable place. Protectors/Controllers are young, unsophisticated parts who are desperate to be helpful but have only crude tools at their disposal. They will do whatever seems necessary to keep us safe, including denying access to any natural gifts.

Other primary subpersonalities emerge and thrive as the child grows, each also operating as a kind of protector and controller: for example, a Pusher, who wants to get things done (starting with walking and talking); a fledgling Inner Critic, who observes how well we're following the family rules and rebukes us for lapses; or an Inquisitive self, who blossoms when Mom and Dad praise their toddler's curiosity. A different family might reinforce a Stoic self, who doesn't ask questions (so that, in time, this subpersonality becomes a primary self) and might squash the eagerness of an Inquisitive self by dismissing it as "too nosy" or "rambunctious," so that it is quickly buried in the unconscious and becomes a hidden self.

Some emerging selves are nipped in the bud. If a youngster tests the boundaries of self-expression by throwing temper tantrums and these outbursts are met with reprimands, she may bury her anger, dissatisfaction, or disagreeableness — perhaps so deeply that she loses awareness of ever having had those feelings. But they're still there. She'll still have a hidden Angry self, a Dissatisfied self, a Disagreeable self, and others that are unacknowledged.

I don't want to oversimplify; the human psyche is, of course, wonderfully complex. Kids are resilient, and families are multifaceted. Not all hidden selves are necessarily shut down completely by family dynamics. For example, Mom may frown when her toddler disobeys, but a free-spirited aunt may be delighted by his defiance. The child files away that opposite response, and as a teenager, when he begins exploring his blossoming Sensual and Sexual selves, he may turn to his aunt as a confidante.

Like this mother and aunt, siblings may develop very different primary and hidden selves in reaction to the same upbringing. One sister may grow up like her reserved, self-effacing mother, finding comfort in meeting obligations; another sister may feel confined by duty and predictability and instead crave drama and surprises.

In fact, it's not unusual for primary selves to form in opposition to parental approval — a Nonconformist or a Wild Child. The son of a neat freak may develop an Inner Slob as a way of asserting independence and individuality. Conversely, a man raised in a messy, chaotic home may lead with subpersonalities who are reliable, punctual, and tidy, such as an Order Lover.

Parent-approved primary selves aren't necessarily all sweetness and light, either. Some parents reward cantankerousness and nudge cooperative selves into dormancy. Maybe cynicism and toughness were valued in your home or neighborhood, and you learned that being emotionally receptive invited harm. In that case, you'd disown your softer selves.

Most moms and dads don't set out to be wanton squelchers of a child's inner selves. They're trying to be good parents, a job that requires discouraging certain selves — say, the self who poops in his pants, the self who bonks a playmate over the head with a toy truck, or the self who wants to eat chocolate for every meal. A functioning family — and a functioning culture — requires that some inner selves be controlled. The line between socializing a kid and repressing her vital parts is a fine one. Some parents go overboard because that's what their parents did (or didn't do). Your parents' responses to you are shaped by their life experiences, expectations, preconceptions, disappointments, doubts, beliefs, longings, unlived dreams, and, notably, their own inner selves — which in turn were formed in reaction to feedback they got from their parents. When you first met your relatives, you were essentially introduced to a family tree of inner selves.

The motivation of every self, primary and hidden, soft and harsh, is to protect your vulnerability. Each one has a gift. People sometimes give insulting names to the parts they know, like Madame Insatiable, Lazy Lout, or Neal's Loser. But renounced selves aren't always destructive or monstrous. A great many of our hidden alter egos — suppressed by parents unequipped to handle them — are kickass (that is, terrific). You will learn how to turn creative, resourceful members of your inner world — like a hidden Dreamer, Visionary, Gambler, or Avenger — into valuable allies who can help you cross your finish line.

Growing New Selves

Major milestones such as the birth of a sibling, starting school, the hormonal surges of adolescence and menopause, marriage, parenthood, the death of a parent, or a medical diagnosis (as well as transformative experiences like activating the final eighth process) naturally stimulate the growth of new alter egos throughout our lives. Sometimes a crisis moves you to create a self — or to get familiar with selves you already have and engage them as allies.

Another way subpersonalities develop is through conscious cultivation. In college, I had a primary self system (a term I didn't know at the time, of course) that included a Risk Taker and Wild Dancer, both admired by my friends. But I was tormented by another part — years later, I named this hidden self the Great Silencer — who turned me completely tongue-tied when I was around a guy who was interested in me. After one particular evening, when I literally bored the passion out of my date and felt powerless to stem the rising tide of indifference, I vowed to never be boring again. I conjured an alter ego who could speak easily and charmingly, no matter how nervous I was. I patterned this fake-it-till-you-make-it self (whom I came to call Social Grace) after my roommate, an expert in romance.

Sophia's Selves

To help identify the subpersonalities that might be hindering her from making a decision about her relationship with John, Sophia kept an inner self diary for a day, making a note whenever she felt a particular subpersonality operating in her life, and giving a quick description of the situation. The goal of this practice is to notice your alter egos, whether or not you like them. In our next session, Sophia pulled a small spiral notebook from her purse. "Okay," she said, opening it with a flourish. "Here's my Selfie Report."

> I started Thursday with many of my primary selves. One is Extra Helpful self, who got up extra early and made pancakes for John because he'd worked extra late the night before. He was happy, and I felt good about that. I also left for school extra early, because my Pusher's to-do list was so long. I fed our classroom hamsters and tortoise, put up a new bulletin board, went over my lesson plans, and got everything ready for the kids. I was a Responsible Adult with a sprinkle of Superwoman. I spent too much time on the bulletin board — that was my Perfectionist. And maybe my Artist too. I love how it looks.
>
> All day I was in my alter ego of Nice-but-Don't-Mess-with-Me Teacher. Everything went well. There was a strange moment at morning recess: Some sixth graders were bullying a boy, Barry, in my class — kind of a shy, geeky kid. My Justice Seeker charged out, and I intervened. Afterwards Barry looked so hopeless that I suddenly felt like crying. That's my Compassionate

self, for sure. But he's also so ineffectual at sticking up for himself that for a split second I also felt like slugging him. That's a hidden self. Did he trigger my Inner Bully? My brothers would probably agree that I can be a browbeater. That's difficult to acknowledge.

When I left, around dinner time, I locked my keys in the car — let's call that self the Exhausted self. I had to call John to bring the extra set of keys. He was nice about it, but he teased me, very gently, and out came my Raging Bull. It was because I felt so stupid and I was so tired. And hungry too! But I immediately reined in the Raging Bull, and I spent the rest of the night being Extra Helpful self, especially in the bedroom, if you know what I mean. I guess I started and ended the day with the same Extra Helpful self, but doing different things. Then I realized John has an almost perfect Extra Helpful self when I need him!

And that made me feel worse, because I felt guilty because he's so good and I'm so bad. At least according to my Inner Critic, who kept attacking me for being stupid and behaving badly, saying over and over that I'm mean and don't deserve John's loving kindness, that I'm a stupid idiot for locking my keys in my car. That's a self I don't like — my Stupid Idiot self. Although they were strong and they were there, I did not express them. Just before we fell asleep, John brought up marriage in a kind of jokey way, but I felt like "I can't think about another thing — let alone that!" Luckily, I was too tired to do anything other than say we'd talk about it later, and off to sleep we went. I was so exhausted even my Inner Critic couldn't give me insomnia.

I asked Sophia to describe each of these selves, noting its function, its key to success (the rule or rules it believes must be followed), and the advantages (the gift) and disadvantages (the sting) it carries. Here are excerpts from her list:

My Responsible Adult

- **Function:** Aims to please.
- **Key to success:** Play by the rules of polite society — most importantly, *be nice*!
- **The gift:** People like me.
- **The sting:** I sometimes do things I don't want to do — or stop myself from doing something I really want to — because I'm worried about what people will think of me.

My Perfectionist

- **Function:** Needs everything to be just right (from putting up a classroom bulletin board to loading the dishwasher to giving a party to writing a report).
- **Key to success:** Be forever flawless at everything.
- **The gift:** Motivates me to meet my goals. I do a good job.
- **The sting:** Sometimes slows me down because it thinks everything needs a little more work. Can be impatient when people don't do things the way I

know they should be done. Also, I might not try new things because there's a *big* chance I won't be perfect at them.

My Critic

- **Function:** Points out my flaws in the harshest way possible and is 100 percent sure I don't measure up.
- **Key to success:** Be perfect at everything.
- **The gift:** This part keeps me constantly improving. It gets me to the gym!
- **The sting:** Makes me feel really bad about myself and that I'll never measure up. Also, my Critic seems to be able to put together an army of hurting helpers on demand and brings in like-minded selves who believe I should be eternally ideal. That's a powerful sting — practically an electrocution.

My Passionate One

- **Function:** This self fully loves what she loves.
- **Key to success:** Do what you love.
- **The gift:** I feel happy and present when I'm involved in something I love, like teaching or bicycling or good times with John.
- **The sting:** I can get upset when someone close to me doesn't seem to be as passionate as I am. There's another sting too. This part of me can keep me from focusing because when I have too much of Passionate One, everything can be absorbing, and I flit from thing to fascinating thing, which is fine on the one hand, but I can get lost for hours

and not do important things. I guess my Passionate One can be a form of procrastination.

THE FINAL EIGHTH PROCESS
Start a List of Your Different Selves

As you progress on your final eighth journey and read about all kinds of selves, you will start to notice a vast variety of personas.

Think about the selves described in Sophia's diary and how many selves you have that are similar or dissimilar.

Start a list of alter egos in a notebook or computer file. Note the ones that strike your fancy, that you'd like to evolve or cultivate, as well as those that are foreign or even repulsive to you. Think about how they may help or hinder you in achieving your final eighth goal.

THE FINAL EIGHTH PROCESS
Keep an Inner Self Diary

---

1. For at least one or two days, keep an inner self diary. Simply jot down any selves who appear or whose presence you feel. They may or may not visibly express themselves. Identify them to get to know them better, as awareness is power. You might like to keep track for both a workday and a weekend day, as sometimes different alter egos are present in different environments.

2. Describe the circumstances in which these selves appear.

THE FINAL EIGHTH PROCESS
Identify Your Primary Selves

Your list of inner selves and your inner self diary will reflect many alter egos — some you lead with and some you squelch. The next step is identifying your primary selves: the parts of yourself with whom you most identify and are most familiar; the aspects of yourself that you lead with, that define who you are in the world, how you think, and how you behave (and yes, even how you dress). Give each subpersonality a label or name, like the Perfectionist, the Critic, Johnny-Be-Good, or Tough Tess. (Alter egos might be any gender; women may have guy selves, and vice versa, and some selves are genderless or gender-fluid.) Using Sophia's list as a model, add a short description of each primary self's function, the rules for behavior that are its key to success, its gift, and its sting.

CHAPTER

Do It Yourselves

How to Have an Inner Voice Dialogue

*We have all a better guide in ourselves, if we would
attend to it, than any other person can be.*

— Jane Austen, *Mansfield Park*

*How many times have you been mad at yourself
for not listening to your own wisdom and instincts?*

It's time for you to talk to — and *as* — one of your subpersonalities and sort out what it has to say. These inner selves
give you information and insights. Some of what they say may
be surprising, some of it may be exhilarating, and some of it
may be hard to hear, but all of it will be helpful. You might feel
a particular alter ego is being a pain and a drag, holding you
back from your final eighth goal, but from its point of view
it's protecting you somehow. The goal is to be curious about
what's going on with it, not to attack or try to kill it.

35

One of the ways to keep the voice dialogue method safe and effective is to start with a primary self. Your primary selves are the more public alter egos you identify with, the ones that define who you are, how you think, and how you behave. They're the parts who got you the first seven-eighths of the way toward your goal.

In voice dialogue, after deciding which self to dialogue with, you move from the chair you're sitting in to a different spot in the room. There, you speak as your chosen inner self, using the pronoun *I* to refer to that self, and the third person, *she*, *he*, or *they*, to talk about yourself. You start by asking the self some questions, and the self is free to respond by sharing anything that comes up. After this dialogue, you return to the chair where you started and sort out what the subpersonality had to say and how that makes you feel. The chair where you start and finish the process is a place for strengthening awareness. I call it the Aware Chair.

Though it may feel strange at first, embodying a subpersonality using this process is highly effective. When you experience each self as a separate entity, you get a fresh perspective on a distinct problem and on life in general. No subpersonality knows the whole story. As we go through life, the quiet, complicated, or hidden selves can be drowned out by louder, more confident subpersonalities who are sure they're the only ones who truly know who you are and what you should do. You'll feel a palpable shift in your view of yourself when you can switch from saying "I'm a complete screwup" to "In certain situations I feel like I'm taken over by a self who panics or a self who is totally confused." Or shifting from "I'm just a ridiculously timid person" to "A part of me is really scared." It comes as a great relief to learn that each of these selves is only one aspect of your personality and not the whole enchilada.

As a guide, here's an excerpt from Sophia's voice dialogue session with me. I've edited out some of the long silences and hesitations, but it's important to know that a dialogue with a self isn't glib or even especially fluid. Sometimes people find themselves tongue-tied, especially as they're learning this technique. Be gentle with yourself: you learn the process by doing it.

Sophia decided to start with her Passionate One. She moved to a small armchair near my bookcase and began speaking, "I'm Sophia's Passionate One."

Question: Do you have a name?

Answer: You can call me Passion.

Question: When did you become a part of Sophia's life?

Answer: I think when she was in fifth grade. My mom — Sophia's mom — well, I guess she's my mom too — took her to see the *Nutcracker*, and Sophia fell in love with ballet. Or I did. Me, Passion. I wanted to take lessons immediately, and I kept Sophia practicing hard. I love everything about ballet, even learning the French words for steps, like *pas de bourrée* and *assemblé en tournant*. The movements were as beautiful as their names! That was the first time I got Sophia to throw herself into something that really transported her.

Question: What role or function do you serve in Sophia's life?

Answer: I keep her connected to the world. I bring

her excitement and help her enjoy life. I remind her not to take things for granted. I express strong emotion.

Sophia-as-Passion was on the edge of her chair, leaning forward. Her gaze was intense and her expression radiant as she continued.

I make life fun and interesting! I gave Sophia a break from thinking about what Sophia saw as her responsibilities, like worrying about her mother. And her father. He was gone a lot, and then he was gone pretty much for good. He didn't pay too much attention to us.... But he listened sometimes if I was talking about one of my passions, like ballet. Huh. I never thought of that before. Wow.

Question: What rule, or rules, do you think Sophia needs to obey?

Answer: Well, I think I help Sophia know what's important. That's my rule for success. If I'm not passionate, it's not worth doing! I let Sophia be fully present and happy when she's doing what I'm passionate about. If I wasn't around, she might be too fearful. And let's face it, she would not be as attractive. When I'm embodied, I flow with sensuality. Sophia never lets me talk like this. It's so much fun — life is dull if you don't feel things fully.

Question: In terms of her final eighth issue, what do you, Passion, think about John?

Answer: John is patient and kind, but he's not a very

passionate person. I wish he were more passionate. I don't mean sexually, that's all fine. Or maybe I do.

Sophia-as-Passion's eyes widened. "Uh-oh," she said. "I think I just hit a nerve."

At this point, Sophia asked to return to center, to the Aware Chair. She was rattled. I asked her to sit silently and turn her focus inward, to become aware of her emotions, her breathing, and other bodily sensations as the energy of the Passion subpersonality subsided. After sitting quietly for a while, I asked Sophia how she'd felt physically and emotionally when she was speaking as her Passionate self.

"Well, I think my gestures were more graceful and bigger," she said, "and my voice was deeper than usual. As Passion, I took fuller breaths. I sounded more excited about life, and I felt it too. It was fun having her energy. Until she said that thing about John. I don't know why I — she — I said that about sex. That really threw me.

"John and I are sexually compatible; that's always been a good thing. Even when other things are bad. Well, the sex is more comfortable than super-hot or adventurous. And that's totally fine with me. I guess that's less fine with Passion. Passion sounded underwhelmed. But speaking as me, Sophia, from here in the center, where it feels like I have an overview, I think I care less about the sex and more about the fact that he doesn't have any obsessions, no crazy enthusiasms. He's so even-keeled it can be annoying. But I have to admit that it's also a comfort."

We were silent again until I asked whether she had any other observations.

"That thing about my dad," she said. "It's true that one of the few times he paid attention to me was when I showed him what I'd learned in ballet class. Sometimes he'd even be my 'danseur partneur,' and he'd lift me high in the air as I attempted *grand écarts au tour jetés en l'air*, and the occasional cartwheel. We'd both get weak with laughter."

She looked on the brink of tears and quickly shook her head. "I was passionate about my dad. When he left us, it was so painful. A part of me — I guess it was Passion — thought that Dad went away because I didn't hold his interest."

Sophia was solemn for a moment. "Maybe that's why I can get upset and feel rejected when someone doesn't match my level of passion — because I think that means they've lost interest in me. And they will leave. Or at least Passion feels that way."

I offered a quick recap: "So, as you mentioned in your list, part of Passion's sting is that she makes you impatient with people who aren't as passionate as you are, but what you're learning is that underneath the fervor is sensitivity to rejection. And an additional part of her gift is she enlarges your life."

"That sounds right," Sophia said, still sitting centered in the Aware Chair. She thought some more. "Here's something else: My dad was passionate, so maybe I get a little of that from him. Which is kind of scary because he left us to follow his passion." Sophia rolled her eyes. "Her name was Tiffany. Tiffany is who Dad left my mom for. Of course, John would be hurt if I broke up with him. Maybe I'm worried that I'll be mean and hurt people if I follow my passion. Like my dad. Wow. Double wow. Maybe I want to break up with John before he gets bored and breaks up with me. I've already got some pretty amazing new stuff to think about, and we've only talked to one of my inner selves!"

That's one of the best things about learning to use voice dialogue: big, startling, extremely useful insights pop up far sooner than you might imagine. In addition, the act of speaking as and with an inner self is a source of timed-release wisdom that triggers more shifts in the longer term.

Now it's your turn to dialogue with a primary self. This is an exercise you can repeat or come back to at any time.

THE FINAL EIGHTH PROCESS
Voice Dialogue with a Primary Self

Choosing a Self

Choose a spot in the most private area of your living space as your center for the dialogue. This starting place is your Aware Chair. Select a primary self to have a conversation with. It can be one of the primary selves you identified in chapter 2, or you can go with whichever primary self occurs to you. You might pick a self that operates a lot in your life, such as your Professional, Pupil, or Procrastinator. Or you could access an alter ego that's directly involved in your final eighth dilemma or goal.

If you can't decide, go to the self that is having difficulty choosing (perhaps an Inner Perfectionist or Insecure One). Any self you dialogue with has wisdom to offer.

Speaking as a Self

Move to another part of the room and speak as that alter ego. Use the first-person pronoun *I*. Use the third person and your name when referring to yourself in the Aware Chair. For example, my Inner Pusher might say, "Bridgit needs to do more all the time!"

Answer some of the questions below from the point of view of the inner self you've chosen. Keep a record of the dialogue. You can write in your journal or make an audio or video recording. If you like, dive right in and ask questions related to your final eighth issue, or move on to that later, after getting a more general idea of how this subpersonality works in your life. You can come back to this exercise at any time.

Questions for an Inner Self

- Who are you?
- Do you have a name?
- How old are you?
- When did you become a part of [your name]'s life?
- What role or function do you serve in [your name]'s life?
- What rule, or rules, do you think [your name] needs to obey?
- Are you in a particular part of [your name]'s body?
- What is your energy like? For example, is it loose, constricted, wide open, lethargic, frenetic, mellow?
- How do you protect [your name]?
- How do you know what you know? Do you have any role models — someone you know, a friend or a relative, or someone famous whom you've never met?

Or did you learn what you know because you made the decision *not* to behave like a family member or authority figure?

- Whom do you admire?
- What are you good at?
- What do you believe is the key to success?
- How do you define success?
- What has been your greatest success?
- What do you think about the final eighth goal or project that [your name] is close to accomplishing but can't seem to complete?
- How do you keep [your name] from reaching his or her goal, if you do? If you impede progress, why is doing that important to you?
- Is there anything you are afraid of?
- Is there anything else you'd like to add?

Return to Center

After you have considered as many of these questions as you wish (and any others you think of), and the self has responded, return to your Aware Chair for centering and processing.

Centering

Sit in silence for a few minutes. Become aware of your breath, the way your body feels (tight? relaxed? different from the way it did before you spoke as this self?), and your emotional state (calm? alarmed? relieved? different from the way you felt before you expressed yourself as this self?). Note how the energy of the subpersonality shifts and subsides.

Processing

Read over your written responses or review the recording you made. As you review these responses, consider the following questions and reflect on any insights that come up.

- What are the main points of what this self had to say?
- What, if anything, did the self say that surprised you?
- What new information do you have after listening to the self?
- What might be different if you allowed this self to be more (or less) active in your life?
- Did the dialogue inspire any thoughts or revelations about your goal, your stuckness, or your final eighth issue?

This process cultivates overall awareness and develops your nonjudgmental observer, who learns from all the selves. It can lead to important insights about your final eighth issue. You may have an immediate breakthrough, or you may not be sure what you've learned until your answers have cooked for a bit. Review them again a few days after the dialogue and see what else comes up.

No subpersonality is inherently good or bad, even if it screws you up in its effort to protect you. The aim isn't to annihilate or banish a troublesome self but the opposite: to draw it out, get to know it, and ultimately transform the way it operates in your life. Interacting directly with selves — a Debbie Downer, say, or a Law-breaking Lloyd — offers new and essential information about being stuck, about the mysterious inability to achieve a meaningful life goal.

You can repeat this process with different primary parts of yourself, immediately or later. When you're ready to start another dialogue, begin the process again by sitting quietly in your Aware Chair to become centered. Focus for a few moments on the inner self with whom you want to converse. Also, if there seems to be a self particularly related to your stuckness, converse with that self as many times as needed.

At an Impasse?

Sometimes people doing this exercise for the first time blank out. If that happens to you, switch to a different primary self, one that feels more friendly or eager to share.

If you seem to have chosen an alter ego who doesn't communicate verbally, that's okay. Just hang with it. Stay in that energy for several minutes so that you get a physical sense of the self. It might be a silent persona who likes to assess things from behind the scenes. Sometimes nonverbal parts of you eventually begin speaking.

Identify Your Hidden Selves

Who's Stopping You?

Just the mention of these peace-disturbers brings up so much frustration and resistance.

— RAPHAEL CUSHNIR,
Surfing Your Inner Sea:
Essential Lessons for Lasting Serenity

The ability to manage the unknown and tolerate the doubt, uncertainty, chaos, and tentativeness accompanying the realm of the unfamiliar is vital.

In your initial voice dialogue conversations, you learned how to identify and speak with primary parts of yourself. This process helps you see how they operate in your life, as well as how they function in relation to your final eighth frustrations. Regardless of their presentation, subpersonalities — both primary and hidden selves — feel their sacred duty is protecting your vulnerability and helping you avoid rejection. However, since each subpersonality assumes it knows what's best for you despite having only partial information, over time their collective inaccurate perceptions and enforcement methods can become problematic. This is especially true as you challenge yourself to grow by wrestling with your final eighth issue.

Once you're comfortable communicating with your primary selves, it's time to identify some of your hidden selves. These are sometimes also called *disowned selves*, a term coined by Nathaniel Branden, or *shadow selves*, a term Carl Jung used to describe the unknown, dark side of the personality. These are aspects of your personality that were squelched or buried after meeting with parental or societal disapproval. I use the term *hidden*, as I'm referring to the subpersonalities that you'd like to hide or wish away as well as those you haven't even met. You will discover their invisible influence — the force that's keeping you stuck — and shockingly, you may find that they have good reasons for holding you back.

Some of your hidden selves may be difficult to embrace, and some may be delightful, but all will be helpful. A feckless Inner Slacker may dismay and embarrass you, but its gift may be to teach you the importance of letting go of excess responsibility and slowing down to balance your busy life. An Angry self, bristling with barely controlled rage, may, in the right proportion, help you stand up for yourself. The exercises in this chapter will unite you with stimulating and sensual selves as well as smart, smart-ass, and strong parts of your personality. All selves have a gift and a sting, and all have wise counsel to offer.

Hidden selves may be alter egos you're keenly aware of but desperately wish weren't there and often aim to hide, like an

Addict self. This alter ego, like all others, is trying to protect your vulnerability and help you avoid something painful. Although you're quite familiar with this self, you don't want it to exist, nor do you want others to know about it. Let's use the example of a Binge Shopper self. This alter ego costs you a lot in time, energy, and money. At first, you try not to indulge, but at a certain point the Shopper prevails. You might hide your binges by using cash or cash advances for purchases. If this self is uncontrolled, you might run up serious debt and not be able to stop spending. In addition, it saddles you with the burden of having a dirty little secret. Hiding begets more lies, and lies beget more hiding. You might pay for a secret storage unit to hold your purchases, thinking that you will return most of them the next day. But you don't. After acting out and compelling you to buy things you don't need, the subpersonality retreats when the damage is done. And you suffer. This chain of events often causes embarrassment, shame, disappointment, anxiety, fear, depression, and daunting practical ramifications.

Hidden selves can be parts you are truly unconscious of — you don't feel them, and you deny their existence (such as a Greedy or Vengeful self). However, occasionally you're overcome by a forbidden subpersonality, and you lose it out of the blue. When one of these alter egos comes out of hiding, it can feel like something foreign has literally taken you over, which is often scary (to yourself as well as to people around you). After the hidden self behaves badly, it retreats, leaving in its wake guilt, regret, grief, and other painful aftermath emotions and adverse consequences. These could include a bewildering sense of not knowing yourself and not being able to trust yourself.

Don't Negate the Negative

An important goal of voice dialogue is simply to experience a subpersonality as a separate entity, without its being drowned out or otherwise concealed. You may find this uncomfortable, because it's unusual for these hidden parts to be allowed out. In addition, these inner selves are often intense. Acknowledging these alter egos can be painful, but it's often worth the distress, as it can increase our willingness to try new things. As an example, I'll share a highly embarrassing outburst I had at a clinic where I worked a long time ago.

Due to the dictates of my Nice and Scared selves, my general pattern was to stay in situations I should have quit long before. My Pleaser and Perfectionist kept me focused on doing an excellent job. This was a helpful strategy at first, as I accrued many invaluable skills as part of my first seven-eighths. But simmering underneath was a vague awareness of frustration, boredom, and despair, the magnitude of which I did not consciously grasp. I was also aware of fatigue and headaches. What did not register, as it was completely disowned and hidden, was that deep inside I was getting very angry. I didn't realize how much I disagreed with the warped priorities of my department's supervisors. The truth is, I didn't respect them. These highly educated individuals spent an inordinate amount of time distracting themselves with idleness, irrelevance, and insensitivities. Every single quarter, the bosses would act like it was a surprise when the accreditors arrived for their regular site visit, forcing the staff to abandon their clinical work to do hours of busywork that was 100 percent avoidable.

After a long day, as I was racing to leave work for my evening part-time gig (my primary selves include Doer and

Work-Work-Work selves), I suddenly remembered that I hadn't done one last task at the clinic — something I felt shouldn't even be part of my job description. Having worked unpaid overtime once again while the supervisors had long since gone home, I felt a flash of anger as I ran back to get it done.

Suddenly my Raging Bull self erupted and threw folders across the room, starting a cascade of destruction. The files collided with a large glass vase filled with dying flowers on my colleague's messy desk. As it broke, the shards ricocheted into the window and cracked it. Fetid water oozed over my coworker's pile of paperwork.

For a second all I could do was look in disbelief at the mini-Superfund site I'd just created. I'd been running late already. I was incensed as I scurried to find a towel to clean up as best I could in less than a minute. Thoroughly enraged, I ran out of the building and grabbed a cab and snarled the address I needed to get to.

On a scale from 1 to 10, the anger of my Raging Bull was at a level 10. As the cab crawled across town in choked traffic to get to my second job, my rage slowly evaporated. And as my Raging Bull self retreated back into hiding, I felt my vulnerability and began shaking with fear and mortification. How was I going to explain not only the broken vase but the busted skyscraper window? My inner Little Girl was terrified of getting in trouble and being fired. My Good Girl and Nice selves dreaded other people finding out that I'm not so nice all the time. Even worse, my behavior seemed to confirm their worst fear, that I'm really a terrible person.

As my Let's-Assess-This self reviewed what happened, I calmed down. Helping me relax and take a larger view is a major gift of this mature self, which concluded that given the mess I'd created, I had cleaned up pretty well. Also, I had completed the original moronic task that started this unfortunate chain of events. Then this self went into damage-control mode and eventually came up with a good explanation for the wreckage. My Public Relations Doyenne and Poker Face are also members of my Fix-This-Situation team (as are my Inner Machiavelli and my Liar, which is hard to confess). By the time my taxi finally reached my destination, I was only a few minutes late, could see a bit of humor in the fiasco, and was able to focus on my next stint.

In the end, my Fix-This-Situation alter egos triumphed. Not only had I cleaned up well enough that the truth was never discovered, but the damage was covered by insurance. For two weeks the mystery of the broken window gripped the office suite. The glass was replaced in a complex operation executed by a crew of professional high-rise scalers who gained an unexpected contract from my misdeed. (This did make me note the economic benefits from repairs necessitated by destructive outbursts of hidden selves. But I digress.)

But there was a more important consequence. The sting of my Raging Bull was obvious. Its gift was the message that I needed to heed my deep unhappiness at my situation. Humiliating though it was to lose it at the office and have to lie about it, it made me pay attention to my profound dissatisfaction. Not long thereafter, I left the job, of my own accord and on good terms with my employers. My Raging Bull was right. It was time to break out of that barn and graze on new, wide-open pastures!

Learning to identify and describe your hidden inner selves

creates at least a little space between you and the ideas you have about yourself. And that's what we want. At first, you may notice just a pause before your customary reaction (by a self or selves) to an event or an exchange with another person. Ask yourself what happened. Was that a hidden self reacting? Were there numerous subpersonalities with conflicting responses to the situation? Did you feel awkward, vulnerable, ashamed? Proud or secretly proud?

Becoming attuned to experiences like this helps you develop an accepting, nonjudgmental inner observer who learns from all the selves. The final eighth journey is the spectacular shift from comprehending your world through your limited, habitual lenses to expanding your awareness through discovering different points of view from other aspects of yourself. This sometimes dizzying expansion is like an astronaut's view of our globe. It can be unnerving, but also eventually liberating and perhaps even a tad enlightening. At the very least, it's enlivening.

Every self, primary and hidden, offers a gift. Many of these subpersonalities are creative, resourceful members of your inner world who want to influence your outer world. In the following exercise, you'll meet some of your hidden selves.

THE FINAL EIGHTH PROCESS
Keep a Hidden Self Diary

1. For at least one or two days, keep a diary, as you did when you explored your primary selves. Simply jot down the names of alter egos who appear,

or whose presence you feel. They may or may not overtly express themselves. Especially in the case of hidden selves, you can observe what you *don't* do. For example, you might be aware of an insulting part of you that wants to curse someone out, but at the same time you are aware of a stronger part of you that stops you. More than likely one of these selves is primary, and one is hidden. By identifying them, you can get to know them better. Sometimes different alter egos are present in different places, so you might want to keep a diary on a workday and again on a weekend day.

2.   Describe the circumstances in which these different selves appear.

THE FINAL EIGHTH PROCESS
Identify Your Hidden Selves

Your inner self diary will reflect many alter egos — some you lead with and some you squelch. The next step is identifying your hidden selves, the parts you try to hide away and wish weren't there. Give each one a name or label, like the Naysayer or the Super-sensitive, Darlene Dilettante or Debutant Damien. Remember that selves might be any gender or gender-fluid. As you did for your primary selves, add a short description of each self's function, articulating the rule for behavior that is its key to success, its gift, and its sting.

As an example, here's a description of my Raging Bull self:

Function: This self protects me from stagnating.
Key to success: Break things if you have to!
The gift: I am powerful and cannot be ignored.
The sting: This part scares me, as it can be destructive.

5

Dialogue with Your Hidden Inner Selves and Learn Their Secret Wisdom

An inevitable though often ignored dimension of the quest for "wholeness" is that we must embrace what we dislike or find shameful about ourselves as well as what we are confident and proud of.

— Parker J. Palmer, *Let Your Life Speak*

When you finally decide to face your demons, you will also find your angels.

In chapter 4, we worked on identifying your hidden selves, the subpersonalities that you'd like to cover up or wish away. Employing the same voice dialogue process you used to get to know your primary selves, it's now time to interview these shrouded aspects of yourself, which, like your primary selves, each have a gift and a sting. Hidden selves may be unsettling, but they also represent untapped potential. They have important things to tell you about the obstacles preventing you from achieving your meaningful goal. Voice dialogue is a safe and effective method of getting to know these selves.

One reason voice dialogue is so powerful is that embodying the self and allowing it to express itself, *as is*, activates capacities well beyond the logical brain: visual, spatial, auditory, rhythmic, verbal, kinesthetic, and physiological. You experience the felt sense of the growth of your overall awareness. You learn to experience yourself as having a larger presence, embodying multiple, and often opposing, agendas. You can feel the excitement of the prospect of a fuller life while acknowledging that these discoveries may also inspire fear.

Voice Dialogue with Hidden Selves

Here's an excerpt from Sophia's voice dialogue session when she summoned her inner Raging Bull (who is entirely different from my own Raging Bull: all our hidden selves are unique). I've edited out some of the pauses for easier reading. When you do this yourself, your dialogue might be fast and furious at times, but at other times it might be slow and awkward. Be gentle with yourself. You learn the process by doing it.

Remember Sophia's dilemma — to wed or not to wed? That is Sophia's final eighth issue, which she's been struggling with on and off for years. Sophia began in her Aware Chair, and when she was ready to start dialoguing as Raging Bull, she moved to another section of the room.

> **Question:** Who are you?
> **Answer:** I'm Sophia's Raging Bull.
> **Question:** What's your role in Sophia's life?

Answer: I keep her awake, so she doesn't throw away her life by being the good girl all day and into the night. The truth is, I'm angry! Sophia is in her Nice Girl selves all the time. I'm furious. I'm not allowed out anywhere. And sometimes that just makes me fucking explode. I'm not allowed at school where she works — she has to be a *boring, pleasant* role model. And not get fired. Fine! I get that. But I'm not going to let her waste her entire life sucking it up. Her father went and got what he wanted. And what? He's allowed and she's not? What kind of bullshit double standard is that? Sophia's got a lot of oppressive rules she blindly follows. "Be passive." "Be nice." "Whatever you do, don't hurt people's feelings!" Says who? What about Sophia's feelings? Do they count for nothing? Sophia's confusing who I am and what I stand for, with her depressed mother —

Sophia stopped as a fleeting look of shock rippled across her face and her eyes widened. My guess was that an alarmed primary self was checking to see if it was safe to continue. Primary selves are usually nearby, ready to squelch hidden selves and shove them back into the shadows. That has been their job most of their life.

Calmly I offered, "Raging Bull, I understand that you're not condemning Sophia's mother. You're trying to make sense of things."

Sophia-as-Raging-Bull nodded. Often, when selves are on a roll, they don't need to be asked questions, as they're thrilled to share their viewpoints. Sophia-as-Raging-Bull took a few breaths and began again in a mocking, singsong tone that soon ramped up into a bellow:

> Sophia's been such a good girl all her life. Every time her heart gets broken by someone else, she predictably dates John again. Oh, did Sophia forget to mention that? It's like she gets goddamn amnesia. Her primary selves can spin it any fairy-tale "it's all good" way they want. But here's what really happened. She went back to John the second time because Lance, the adventurer she had so much fun with, broke her heart. That's the truth. Does it hurt? Yes. Am I the one hurting her? *No!* I didn't break up with her. Lance did. I'm just helping her not have amnesia. Even though Lance left her for other continents and other women, he woke Sophia up! He ignited her passions. And I'm not letting her have amnesia again.

Dismay streaked across Sophia's face as these buried truths unfurled. To assuage any (absolutely appropriate) fear she was feeling, I said, "I imagine that's never been said out loud before."

Sophia-as-Raging-Bull snorted in agreement and, nostrils flaring, continued.

> Said it? Sophia never even thought it before! I'm figuring this out as I go — now that I'm allowed out of my pen. I'm not out to hurt Sophia. Just

the opposite. I love her. Often, I work alongside some of her other selves like her Rebel self. And also, her Passionate One — when she said sex with John wasn't super-hot, she was right! Being a good caretaker just can't be her whole life! If Sophia's lucky enough to live a long life, what's she going to look back on? Huh? Did ya enjoy your unlived life? Are ya happy that ya listened to your mother's bullshit — that nobody else will want Sophia if she doesn't marry John? I'm so, so, so angry! Sophia's mother used the fact that Lance broke up with her as proof of her undesirability. That's her mother talking about herself! Does she want Sophia to have a depressed life like hers? I think so. There's another painful idea. That's taboo, right? Your mother wants you to *not* be happy? Sophia thinks it's me, Raging Bull, that's hurting her!! I'm just saying what's going on. John isn't a bad guy. So, don't let Sophia misinterpret me as saying he's a bad guy. I'm not against him as a person. But if they get married he's going to lock Sophia into a predictable, passion-free life. And I can't let Sophia settle for that!!

After an inner self expresses itself, it's essential to go back to the Aware Chair for reflection and processing in order to reap the benefits of the wisdom revealed in the session. Sophia sat back wordlessly, tears flowing down her cheeks. I asked her some processing questions, including what thoughts were provoked by the new information she'd gotten from Raging Bull.

"I think I'm sort of in shock. I admit it — that rough stuff Raging Bull said is true. I suppose it's like realizing that my choice is how to manage my pain, right? Breaking up is going to hurt. The question is hurt now or hurt later. And imagine it the other way! If down the line we're married with a kid or two and John leaves me? And wildly, if that happens, people will think it's because I'm a scorned woman. But really I'll be angry at myself because I didn't follow my passions. The truth is John's an incredible man, but he and I have different appetites. Being together isn't fair to either of us, if you look at it this way."

Breaking up permanently was quite an emotional experience, but the serenity Sophia gained from having access to many more parts of herself served both John and Sophia. They agreed to be out of touch for six months and periodically check in as friends after that. Sophia was also able to maintain firm protective boundaries for herself and her own grieving process while being as supportive as she could to her mother, who was distraught over the breakup. For several months she limited in-person visits with her mother. On the phone, if her mother started to say something vicious, Sophia would hang up.

Sophia also started taking ballet and other dance classes, which she adored, and made sure she socialized with friends at least once a week. She felt stronger, more fulfilled, and less afraid than perhaps ever before. This self-assurance aided her professional development, and she spearheaded adding movement and mindfulness classes to her school's permanent curriculum. She was surprised when the impulse to reconnect with her father arose, but she called him, and they are beginning to cultivate a relationship on her terms. She is taking dating slowly and enjoying it.

The great thing about communicating with hidden selves is that these subpersonalities offer new information about why we're stuck. Now it's your turn to talk with a hidden self.

THE FINAL EIGHTH PROCESS
Voice Dialogue with a Hidden Self

Choosing a Self

Choose a spot in the most private area of your living space as your center for the dialogue. This starting place is your Aware Chair. Select a hidden self to have a conversation with. It can be one of the hidden selves you identified in chapter 4, or you can go with whichever hidden self occurs to you. You might pick a self that operates a lot in your life even though you don't like it, such as your Overindulger or Lazy Bones. Or you could access a hidden self who's directly involved in your final eighth dilemma or goal.

Speaking as a Self

Move to another part of the room and speak as that alter ego. Use the first-person pronoun *I*. Use the third person and your name when referring to yourself in the Aware Chair. For example, a self I like to hide, the Blatherer-Who-Talks-Endlessly, might say, "Bridgit needs to know I can't think and can't get right to the point. I'm nervous!"

Answer some of the questions below from the point

of view of the inner self you've chosen, and keep a record of the dialogue. You can write in your journal or make an audio or video recording. If you like, dive right in and ask questions related to your final eighth issue, or move on to that later, after getting a more general idea of how this subpersonality works in your life. You can come back to this exercise at any time.

Questions to Ask an Inner Self

- Who are you?
- Do you have a name?
- How old are you?
- When did you become a part of [your name]'s life?
- What role or function do you serve in [your name]'s life?
- What rule or rules do you think [your name] needs to obey in order to be successful?
- Are you in a particular part of [your name]'s body?
- What is your energy like? For example, is it loose, constricted, wide open, lethargic, frenetic, mellow?
- How do you protect [your name]?
- How do you know what you know? Do you have any role models — someone you know, a friend or a relative, or someone famous whom you've never met? Or did you learn what you know because you made the decision *not* to behave like a family member or authority figure?
- Whom do you admire?
- What are you good at?
- What do you believe is the key to success?

- How do you define success?
- What was your greatest success?
- What do you think about the final eighth goal or project that [your name] is close to accomplishing but can't seem to complete?
- How do you keep [your name] from reaching his or her goal, if you do? If you impede progress, why is doing that important to you?
- Is there anything you are afraid of?
- Is there anything else you'd like to add?

Return to Center

After you have considered as many of these questions as you wish (and any others you think of), and the self has responded, return to your Aware Chair for centering and processing.

Centering

Sit in silence for a few minutes. Become aware of your breath, the way your body feels (tight? relaxed? different from the way it did before you spoke as this self?) and your emotional state (calm? alarmed? relieved? different from the way you felt before you expressed yourself as this self?). Note how the energy of the subpersonality shifts and subsides.

Processing

Read over your written responses or review the recording you made. As you review these responses, consider the following questions and reflect on any insights that come up.

- What are the main points of what this self had to say?
- What, if anything, did the self say that surprised you?
- What new information do you have after listening to the self?
- What might be different if you allowed this self to be more (or less) active in your life?
- Did the dialogue inspire any thoughts or revelations about your goal, your stuckness, or your final eighth issue?

You can repeat this process with different hidden parts of yourself, immediately or later. When you're ready to start another dialogue, begin the process again by sitting quietly in your Aware Chair to become centered. Focus for a few moments on the inner self with whom you want to converse. Also, if there seems to be a self particularly related to your stuckness, converse with that self as many times as needed.

Detecting your hidden selves may disrupt you, disturb you, and leave you feeling a bit dizzy. But whether or not you acknowledge them, these selves greatly affect your life. You might as well get to know them. Letting go of old habits and outdated perspectives creates uncertainty and can be disorienting, but it's worth it.

Hidden Selves: The Distraction Crew

Take a moment to think about times when you hit a wall. What personas escort you off the scene — away from moving toward your final eighth? Perhaps varying Distractor selves (saying "Let's go online, let's organize the sock drawer *now*")? Physical/ Body selves ("I'm tired, I'm hungry, I'm restless, so let's take a break")? Bored selves ("Let's go find something more interesting")? Insecure subpersonalities ("It's not worth it, so let's give up, let's drop this, let's move on")? Apathetic selves ("Who cares?")? Do you recognize any of these? Do you have others?

Uncover Your Core Negative Beliefs

Your Invisible Rule Book

How could anyone ever tell you you were anything less than beautiful?

How could anyone ever tell you you were less than whole?

— LIBBY RODERICK, "How Could Anyone"

Discover and discard the deceptions you unwittingly digested.

Congratulations on how much you've unearthed thus far. Maybe starting this journey has already led to your taking steps toward your final eighth goal. The next task in your personal archaeological dig is tracing how your internalized familial and cultural values and rules congealed into unconscious negative beliefs, and how these beliefs are enacted by varying personas and enforced by your Inner Critic and its cadre to make up your worldview.

Very early in life, as primary selves are growing stronger

69

and hidden selves are going underground, we enshrine important messages from our parents — family credos both spoken and unspoken. These injunctions, intended to protect our vulnerability and help us avoid rejection, become core beliefs — one or two foundational assumptions about ourselves and the world that govern our actions and inactions. Even though it's not the goal of most parents, these assumptions often generate a skewed, negative worldview by which many of our subpersonalities operate. According to Clifford Nass and Corina Yen, coauthors of *The Man Who Lied to His Laptop*, there are physiological, psychological, and even evolutionary reasons why negative messages are cemented deeper in our psyche than positive ones. Because we are wired to avoid danger, negative information and its resultant heightened emotions demand more attention from the brain than positive ones. It takes work to move away from your default protective setting of negativity and toward a more positive approach.

Core Negative Beliefs and the Inner Critic

You may not think you have a core negative belief, but if you're mysteriously stuck, one or two ideas are probably holding you back — or blowing you off course and away from your final eighth finish line — without your even realizing it.

"I'm worthless." "I am unlovable." "I am fundamentally flawed." "I'm broken." These are examples of truly believed, yet *false*, painful core beliefs, the foundation on which many people unconsciously base their lives. A person can have a core negative belief and still have many positive attributes.

A core negative belief is different from acknowledgment

of a negative situation. Sometimes it's true that someone you love doesn't love you back; that you're the one who screwed up the math, invalidating the results in a report; that your genius ability to diagram sentences is irrelevant, and perhaps even an impediment, in the era of social media. Experiences like this can hurt, but the difference between them and a core negative belief is that the latter is a hurtful lie that undermines your entire being and destroys your motivation. It is part of the glue that's keeping you stuck.

The concept of core negative beliefs has its roots in cognitive behavioral therapy (CBT), a therapeutic approach originally developed by Albert Ellis in the 1950s and extended by Aaron Beck in the 1960s. Both psychologists noticed that people's feelings are affected less by the external circumstances they face than by the underlying assumptions that shape their perceptions of those circumstances. Many of us routinely maintain unexplored and distorting cognitive biases that we regard as the obvious truth, like "Nothing works out" or "I am ugly" (or inferior, stupid, unlucky, or weak). These cognitive biases are self-reinforcing and all-consuming. It can feel impossible to accept that they are not only separate from our identity but bald-faced lies that have influenced a lifetime's decision-making and behavior. When we're stuck, it's often a signal that we're trapped by the gravitational pull of our core negative beliefs.

People have only one or two core negative beliefs, but they affect everything we think and do. They're like a black hole in space, getting heavier and stronger as it draws in all the matter around it. They limit our access to our full range of intelligence. One of the worst consequences is that they lead us to believe we see the entire situation clearly, blinding us to the fact that our core negative beliefs obstruct and warp our view.

These beliefs are based on ideas and rules instilled by our early caregivers and authority figures: parents, grandparents, babysitters, teachers, and religious and cultural leaders. As mentioned in chapter 2, these caregivers have rules for what kind of person they want you to be. The rules are intended to protect your vulnerability (and theirs). Ideally, they're also intended to help you become a strong, happy, contributing member of society.

Core negative beliefs develop out of rules and commands like "Don't be selfish," "Don't be stupid," "Be quiet," "Be loyal," "Boys are strong," and "Don't cry." Over time, especially when uttered in mean or threatening tones, these edicts can make kids feel they are condemned to be perpetual failures, as opposed to making the occasional blunder. Other such sayings include "A fool and his money are soon parted," "You made your bed, now you must lie in it," "Don't get too big for your britches," and "It's time to give up that pipe dream." You get the picture. What were some of the sayings you grew up with?

In the right quantity, rules and credos reinforce important and healthy values. It's important for kids to learn to control impulsivity, to be accountable and considerate of others. They also need to learn basic rules of social behavior: it's totally reasonable to expect a preschooler to be able to wash their hands and say please.

Very early in a child's development, the precocious Inner Critic absorbs all this cautionary information and takes on the role of enforcing these internalized rules. "Like a well-trained

CIA agent," Hal and Sidra Stone observe, "the Inner Critic… infiltrate[s] every portion of your life, checking you out in minute detail for weakness and imperfections." Also, as they observe in *Embracing Our Selves*, the Inner Critic "has a great talent for teamwork."

The Inner Critic is a five-star general who recruits Protectors/Controllers, Perfectionists, Pushers, Incomparable Comparers, and many other inner selves to enforce the rules it believes are crucial to the individual's survival. A gift of the Inner Critic can be that it gets things done. A sting can be that it's too harsh and thus paralyzes you.

In punitive households where mistakes aren't allowed and kids are yelled at and scolded, they may come to believe that they *deserve* pain. When children are shamed, severely punished, or mocked when they miss the mark or disobey, they start to perceive themselves as fundamentally flawed and irredeemably bad. This perception is the essence of core negative beliefs.

The Inner Critic emerges in this environment to save the child from abandonment. Even if its modus operandi becomes toxic, its original motivation, like that of all our inner selves, is protective. The scar tissue around the primal wounding from criticism forms at a very early stage of development. This is why these beliefs are often brutally fierce and don't respond to logic.

For many of us, as Hal and Sidra Stone note, "At some point the Critic oversteps its bounds, takes matters into its own hands, and begins to operate on its own agenda.…With the Critic's original aims and purposes forgotten, all that is left for it is the excitement of the chase and the wonderfully triumphant feeling of conquest, as it operates secretly and independently of any outside control."

An overzealous Inner Critic can also develop as a result of events like an illness, accident, or death in the family. For example, Melissa grew up with a parent who struggled heroically with a debilitating neurological disorder. Melissa suffered from low-level depression that invariably made her energy fizzle. Every time she started a project, she soon lost motivation and focus, and the goal languished in the final eighth zone. Through the final eighth process, Melissa realized she had a form of survivor's guilt. She became aware that she'd always felt guilty that, in contrast to her disabled mother, she was agile and enjoyed her good physical health. That feeling grew until she felt shame when experiencing any form of enjoyment. The fallout from Melissa's core negative belief ("I don't deserve") was that she unconsciously forbade herself any victory laps. The best way to avoid celebrating victory was simply not to achieve a goal. Melissa had permission from her Inner Critic to go pretty far — seven-eighths of the way there — but not to triumphantly cross the finish line. Even though it was uncomfortable to be stuck, her shrouded priority was to avoid the awful feeling of guilt for achieving and enjoying her success. Even though nobody else ever asked her to limit herself, this was Melissa's unconscious act of distorted loyalty to her mother.

Another tricky characteristic of core negative beliefs is their ability to hide. For example, your Can-Do self may take over your schedule and accomplish many tasks for some time. But if your root belief (conscious or unconscious) is "Nothing works out," different personas will take over and collude to make sure things *don't* work out. Many of us work against ourselves. Failure can truly be an inside job.

We're complicated beings with multiple, competing inner agendas. Once you see what those are and how they're working, you can do something about them.

Your one or two core negative beliefs are an invisible carpet. If your core belief is "Nothing works out," you'll stand on that rug regardless of where you are and what you are doing. When you mistakenly assume something is true, the misconception rules your behavior.

When you're so close to the finish line that your core negative belief is threatened, any number of discomforts roll in. Perhaps you suddenly have to deal with deadlines you completely forgot about, or you feel confused, unfulfilled, irresponsible, overextended, overwhelmed, underwhelmed, fatigued, apathetic, demoralized, irritable, bored, hopeless, or unable to concentrate. Perhaps you're overcome by a headache, toothache, heartache, stomachache, or other aches. Negative beliefs can operate clandestinely and hide behind extreme feelings, vulnerability, and difficult emotions, including shame and envy. The intensity lurking within the negative beliefs triggers avoidance behaviors. You start distracting yourself with fleeting pleasures like Googling rare illnesses, napping, and my favorite — watching all the videos ever made by Missy Elliott and comparing them to the works of Cardi B and Nicki Minaj.

The resulting inaction on your project triggers the false feedback loop that being stuck is proof of the accuracy of your core negative beliefs. Remember, these negative beliefs are lies.

What *is* true is that they exist, and they shape your thoughts, behaviors, attitudes, motivations, and interpretations of natural glitches and frustrations. For many people, these imperatives evolve into silent, powerful, soul-crushing mantras that paralyze rather than motivate.

This Is Not Logical

Tyrone is a newly married, well-liked man in his thirties who felt stuck in his position in the purchasing department at an electronics company. Twice in the past year he had been bypassed for promotions for which he felt qualified.

"It's really frustrating. I'm stressed out and have the energy of an old man! I put in long days and work very hard, and frankly, I need the money a promotion would give me."

Tyrone identified and communicated with several primary selves, including Superhero, Team Player, the Martyr, and Mr. Guilt. Although he had high blood pressure and knew he should try to avoid stress, these primary selves made sure he took care of everyone else first, at the office as well as in his large extended family. Even though it depleted his resources (and caused fights with Angie, his wife), Tyrone always gave more time and money than he could afford whenever his father had a medical appointment or a family member needed an emergency loan (which was rarely paid back).

As Tyrone's awareness of his inner selves grew through voice dialogue, he met his inner Mr. Angry, a hidden self he was aware of but tried to avoid and certainly tried to hide.

"I don't like to admit it — after all, I live via my Superhero a lot — but Mr. Angry scares me. Also, it was wild to discover

I have a hidden part that operates by shutting myself down — Mr. Turn-Out-the-Lights-and-Lock-the-Door-because-There-Is-Nobody-Home! I really didn't know I had that self in me! My wife definitely knew. She'd beg me to not shut down, and I would just tell her she's crazy. Sometimes when I'm in that mode Angie starts yelling at me, 'Where are you?' It's hard to accept I have a Shut-Down self. I got it from my mother. When things around the house got chaotic and Dad was out-of-control drunk, she would just be quiet, still as a mouse. It makes me feel better to know the mission of my Mr. Turn-Out-the-Lights-and-Lock-the-Door-because-There-Is-Nobody-Home — like all the selves — is to protect me. Also, I guess, to protect whoever I'm around so I don't lose control and express my anger. If I do, my Inner Critic has a field day."

"Think about what sayings and clichés you grew up with."

"Put your money where your mouth is!" Tyrone answered immediately. "And there's more…let me think."

Tyrone admired his father, Paco, who immigrated to the United States from the Dominican Republic before finishing high school and went immediately to work. He's still the superintendent in the building where Tyrone grew up. Tyrone felt he owed Paco a debt of gratitude for making it possible for him and his siblings to get an education that had been inaccessible to his dad. Paco prided himself on practicing what he preached, often working alongside his laborers when painting and doing other maintenance operations. As an employee, Paco was dependable, effective, and respected by both the tenants and the landlord.

All of this is admirable, so what was the catch? Tyrone's dad subscribed to the philosophy that "Just when you're about to get ahead, life throws a curveball." Difficult circumstances did indeed occur. But the learned helplessness behind the "life never works out" mentality often left his father depressed and resentful, feelings he tried to ameliorate through binge drinking. He would rage at the injustice of his hard work never leading to financial security. The bouts of drinking caused Tyrone's mother, Emely, to move out and eventually divorce her husband. Paco felt absolutely betrayed, and her departure cemented his outlook that efforts don't reap their just rewards and life doesn't work out. This distressing legacy obviously affected Tyrone, who struggled with many issues, including irrational, powerful guilt.

"I know Mr. Guilt very well! If I don't do what he says, I even get sick sometimes. It's easier to just say yes — no matter how tired I am, or broke. To be clear, Mr. Guilt isn't mean to me. He doesn't have to be. He simply recalls that absolutely everything I have comes from the sacrifices my father made. Without him I would not have the opportunities I'm blessed with. I don't blame either of my parents for the divorce. They were both hurt, and they stayed committed to being good parents. It's my Mr. Guilt, not my parents, who want to make sure I don't take anything for granted."

Tyrone explored the underlying messages of the sayings he grew up with (an exercise presented at the end of this chapter). Here's an excerpt from what he wrote:

> I appreciate the values my father had and wanted us to have. I honor his history of having to leave the Dominican Republic, his country he loved! But felt it did not love him back. There weren't opportunities to build a

life he wanted. For him, "Put your money where your mouth is" and "Practice what you preach" are about being honest and not being corrupt or a hypocrite. "Do honest work for honest pay." "Be a stand-up guy." And the other ones, "Just when you're about to get ahead, life throws a curveball," and "Nothing works out,"…I guess they show that he feels like a victim. That makes me feel so bad for him and makes me feel that I have no right to complain. Zero. Given everything my parents went through, especially my dad, I just owe them a debt of gratitude.

Tyrone realized his core negative belief was that he was undeserving: he felt he hadn't earned his many privileges. The opportunities he had had, for which his father had sacrificed, always made Tyrone feel indebted, and this unconscious stance put him in the position of feeling inadequate. As a result, regardless of circumstance, he put everyone ahead of himself. He began to see how the core negative belief "I don't deserve" and his feeling of indebtedness played into most of his decisions, minor and major. If almost anybody needed anything, he would jump to their aid and skip the gym despite his health issues. He would be too available to his staff and not use his time effectively.

Tyrone began to realize that his need to do everything himself was linked to his dad's credo of practicing what he preached. He valued his reputation of being a team player at work, without embodying his ambition to be a manager eventually. He didn't understand that being a productive team member doesn't mean doing someone else's tasks for them. Tyrone had read a few books on being more effective at work and tried several techniques like goal setting and five-year plans. These are wonderful tools, but if they operate around your distorted reality, they will serve the core negative belief and not your liberated truth.

Here's the exercise Tyrone used to uncover his core negative beliefs. You can return to it as often as you need to.

THE FINAL EIGHTH PROCESS

Uncover Your Core Negative Beliefs

Write down a few of the adages, clichés, or sayings you grew up with. Some of these might be common sayings, and others might be distinctive to your household. If any of them are direct insults, they might actually be your core negative beliefs.

Highlight the parts of the sayings that may represent your core negative beliefs. Condense them to one or two negative beliefs.

What is the underlying message of each saying?

If the above exercise doesn't inspire you, another direct line to your core negative beliefs is letting your Inner Critic tell you what is (allegedly) wrong with you. By now, you're familiar with the process of talking to your inner selves, but I'll review it briefly here.

A dialogue with a self involves three basic steps.

1. Get centered by sitting quietly in the Aware Chair. Focus briefly on your Inner Critic.

Move to another part of the room to speak as the Inner Critic. Record the dialogue (using whatever recording method you've chosen). Start with some of the questions below, and also let the Inner Critic speak spontaneously.

- Do you have a name, or do you just go by Inner Critic?
- What's wrong with [your name]?
- How do you know what you know? Do you have any role models — either someone you know, a parent, grandparent or someone you don't?
- What kind of sayings did you grow up with?
- What do you believe is the key to success?
- What are the rules [your name] should be following?
- Do you know what [your name]'s core negative belief is?
- How do you protect [your name]?
- Is there anything you're afraid of?
- What do you think about [your name]'s final eighth situation?

2. Return to your Aware Chair and get centered. Sit in silence for a few minutes. Focusing within, become aware of your breath, the way your body feels, and your emotional state. Note how the intensity of your Inner Critic starts to fade, and you feel more grounded.

3. Process the dialogue with your Inner Critic while in the Aware Chair by reviewing your record of it. Note any reflections or insights that come up. Highlight

specific words and phrases that expose your core negative beliefs. Condense them into one or two negative beliefs.

What is the underlying message of each saying? What rules are you obeying that cause you to limit your options and make your core negative beliefs come true (as opposed to your cherished final eighth goal)?

Alternative Exercise

If you still can't figure out your core negative belief(s), try this (I always got options!).

Notice your inner dialogue throughout the day. Catch yourself in mid-thought. You might want to set your cell-phone alarm to go off every half hour and quickly jot down what you're telling yourself at that moment. Which self is talking or acting? Later, go through your notes and highlight any negative words or comments and identify your core negative belief.

CHAPTER

7 Twisted Loyalties

Trapped in Your Double Bind

Sometimes the dissonance between reality and false beliefs reaches a point when it becomes impossible to avoid the awareness that the world no longer makes sense. Only then is it possible for the mind to consider radically different ideas and perceptions.

— MARK ENGEL, in the preface to
Steps to an Ecology of Mind by Gregory Bateson

Uncovering your double bind and its function unlocks access to your strengths and submerged creative potential. Carl Jung refers to these hidden qualities as our golden shadow.

If you're stuck, it's likely because your final eighth achievement conflicts with your perception of yourself shaped by your detrimental core negative beliefs, which are the unconscious foundation of your current identity. The root of your stuckness is that accomplishing the goal — from finding love to digitizing the family photos to starting your own business — is in direct conflict with your internal sense of who you are, which is aligned with your skewed worldview. Many people try to feel better by practicing techniques like positive visualization and actively engaging in terrific spiritual and mindful modalities — and then blame themselves for not doing it correctly when negativity and pessimism return. Putting a Band-Aid mantra, like "All is love," on top of a corrosive underlying viewpoint, like "I'm worthless," doesn't work. How can all be love when you're unlovable? It can't.

The contradiction between your final eighth goal and your core negative belief creates a double bind, forcing you to a standstill. The immovable object (your final eighth goal) meets the unstoppable force (your internal sense of yourself, built on your *false* negative belief). Rather than doubling down on your same old ineffective strategies, which tighten the clutch of your double bind, you will learn how to release it.

You've been exploring parts of yourself in order to uncover the mystery of your stalled ass. That got your attention, right? Good, because having a cohesive identity, the felt sense of who you are, is never casual. When that identity is jeopardized, it's perceived as a threat to your very existence, and you plunge into fight-flight-freeze mode. Your final eighth exertions activate and tighten your double bind, which is formed by the parts of you that support your core negative belief and the opposing parts that support and believe in your final eighth goal. This conflict creates extreme feelings of inner discord.

Your core belief defines who you are, but at the same time you're desperate for it *not* to be true. If your core belief is "I'm worthless!," you dread the possibility that you'll do something that proves it. This paradox is what motivates you — and paralyzes you. Different parts of you react to the belief and the fear in different ways.

One of the best-kept secrets of your Inner Critic is that it plays both sides of the double bind. It tells you you're not good enough as it pushes you to be better. It beats you down with your core negative belief while it also flogs you to succeed. Under the unwavering glare of this omnipotent Inner Critic, different selves like Perfectionists and Pushers spring into action to prove the core negative belief untrue by trying to excel at every endeavor. As chief enforcer, the Inner Critic mobilizes all its troops to constantly remind you to improve, meet high standards and expectations, and move toward your goal. This is its way of being supportive and believing in you. And it often seems to bear fruit: accomplishments accrue, and people make significant progress toward their final eighth objective. But the long-term effect of many Inner Critics is downright undermining. Hal and Sidra Stone remind us that when dealing with Inner Critics, "it is so important to go beyond the details of content to experience the energy operating. If someone is sticking a knife into us and, at the same time, talking to us very reasonably about our shortcomings, it might be more advisable to focus on the knife rather than the words."

What Is a Double Bind?

The final eighth makes you bigger, and thus exposed and vulnerable. The sociologist Gregory Bateson defines the double bind as an intense psychological situation that has many layers of constriction, where a person is confronted with two irreconcilable demands or has to make a choice between two undesirable courses of action. An example of irreconcilable demands is divorced parents asking their eight-year-old to choose between Daddy and Mommy. It's a devastating situation that leaves scars. Two undesirable courses of action offer us a vicious illusion of choice. A classic example is from the book *Sophie's Choice*, when a concentration camp guard forces Sophie to "choose" which of her two children to give up to certain death.

When a double bind is encountered early in life, it becomes invisible. The lack of awareness, as well as the inability to articulate this harrowing dynamic, makes you think, wrongly, that something is fundamentally defective about you: that is, you fully accept your core negative beliefs. Later, discomfort around the obstruction of your beloved final eighth project exposes your double bind. You simultaneously want to do it, and you can't.

Double Binds in Action

Babies are born to love and connect. This is delightful. It also serves an essential survival strategy: attachment. Without bonding, without instilling feelings in caregivers to feed, protect, and love the baby, it will most likely die. For the sake of survival, children are faithful to negative messages instilled by their parents and caregivers. Over time, and without our knowledge or consent, our Inner Critics may take over the role of those demanding caregivers.

What might this process look like? Meet Colleen. Like most children, she grew up loving her parents and wanting to please them. Unfortunately, Colleen lived in a stressed home with secrets she was told not to share: that her brother had been diagnosed with autism, and her parents struggled to accommodate his needs and meltdowns. She complied. However, by prioritizing her parents' wishes to keep their tribulations private, Colleen negated her own need for support to handle the family situation. Aiming for approval and trying to foster peace, Colleen went into survival mode and disowned her anger, power, and vulnerability. These constricting priorities thwarted her natural path of growth as she focused on following the rules, being as good and nice as possible, and causing no trouble for her parents.

This act of loyalty put Colleen in the role of parentified child. This concept, introduced by Salvador Minuchin, a luminary in the field of family therapy, involves a role reversal in which a child takes care of the emotional needs of the parent. Instead of being supported by the parents to play, explore, and discover their own preferences, the child focuses on what the parents need and tries to give it to them. Some children try to not have any needs at all. This situation sets the child up to fail: of course a child cannot parent a parent. And all humans have needs. Being cast in the role of emotional caregiver to your caregivers leads to feelings of inadequacy that can become a sinkhole of shame, anxiety, guilt, depression, and learned helplessness.

In short, Colleen ended up disowning her needs, her natural impulses, and her curiosities in order to take care of her mother. This phenomenon is not unusual. Colleen developed a series of primary selves that include a Good Girl, a Pleaser, a Don't-Have-Needs self, and her overseer, an Inner Critic.

Colleen also has a Silent self (whose modus operandi is to say nothing) and a Liar self (who gives the impression to the outside world that all is well).

From her first daycare experience, Colleen enjoyed school. When she got home, she disappeared into her bedroom to read and do homework. This safe haven distanced her from the screaming and banging between her brother and her mother, whom she was never sure how to help. When she tried to intervene, her mom would snarl, "Mind your own business. Concentrate on being a good student, so at least someone in the house can make me proud." This in turn enraged her brother, who understood their mother's insult despite his disabilities. He would howl in agony and taunt and menace Colleen.

Colleen's overwhelmed mother was often angry, frustrated, and impatient with her. Colleen quickly learned that she couldn't rely on her mom. Neither did she want to add to her mom's troubles, so she stopped asking for help. She concentrated on not having needs. This had the effect of making her feel incapable, fueling her core negative belief.

In addition, Colleen unconsciously came to link academic success with making her struggling brother feel even worse about himself, which in turn made her feel terrible. Given the intensity of the mixed messages she was receiving, it's no surprise that Colleen often got low grades, despite her active class participation and exemplary homework assignments. Doing poorly was an act of loyalty. Choosing against herself sealed her attachment to her core negative belief that she was bad. Colleen did well enough to not cause trouble but did not excel, despite her academic potential.

Colleen's predicament was further camouflaged by the

fact that because her brother worked with a special education team, other family members, friends, and professionals mistakenly assumed the family's problems were being adequately addressed. Reinforcing the power of the double bind is the fact that not only is the family unaware of it, but the outside world often doesn't have a clue either, so nobody intervenes. Since the dynamics of the double bind are invisible, the child comes to the conclusion that something must be wrong with them.

As tough as an overtly dysfunctional home is to grow up in, the problems are often obvious — which is a good thing. An example is a parent who hits his kids when drunk. Reactions by members of the family, as well as by the outside world, convey that this behavior is problematic and unacceptable. From Dad's point of view, when inebriated he may feel he's being taken over by his hidden subpersonalities and may feel remorse after a binge. Children in this household can still love their dad, but they realize something is wrong with *his* conduct, as opposed to something being wrong with *them*. In all cases, this type of situation is traumatic and needs serious healing, but the abuse is less confusing. By contrast, when you're locked in a double bind, everything is nebulous and hidden.

Arrested Development

The pain associated with the double bind is mistakenly identified as proof of the core negative belief. Colleen wasn't able to grieve the hardships she and every member of her household endured. She couldn't help her brother get better, couldn't soothe her mother's jangled nerves, couldn't cheer up her father. More heartbreaking yet, she used these facts to fortify her core negative belief: that the situation must be her fault, because she was bad. In doing so, tragically, she colluded in her own arrested development. Although it might be difficult to understand how living an unfulfilled life is a form of loyalty, it's more common than you might think and can contribute to final eighth stuckness.

This built-in complicity is a form of Stockholm syndrome, when there is a psychological alliance between the one in power and the victim because they both adhere to the same core negative beliefs. These dynamics may be entrenched because they have played out in previous generations. (Helping yourself by releasing yourself from your double bind alters your family legacy!) The shackles of the double bind can make you like a bird with only one working wing. Instead of flying toward your goal, you continue to circle back toward your core negative belief.

Your Loyalty Distorts Your View

I have a searing example of stopping my progress cold in my cherished final eighth goal. I was unknowingly loyally bound to my painful core negative beliefs, which were that I was stupid and untalented, and therefore worthless. It's still painful to think about, although it was one of the many experiences that ultimately led to my unearthing the final eighth phenomenon.

Here's what happened. In the early 1990s I pursued an acting career in New York City and juggled many freelance jobs to pay my bills. In any spare moments I had, I worked on my original TV script, called "Mudders," a comedy about a newly divorced mother who moves from New York City to Florida and becomes a Monster Truck champion. I dreamed of selling it to a production company and ideally starring in it as well. This motivation took me through my first seven-eighths, leading to my final eighth, when I finished my script.

This milestone ushered in an exciting new first eighth. I rushed to the far West Side of Manhattan and registered "Mudders" with the Writers Guild. This made it official: I was a writer! I was so happy, thrilled, elated — and did I say happy? I was bursting to share my good news. To hear the sweet words "Way to go, Bridgit," and "Tell me all the details — I want to hear absolutely *everything*," and "When can I read it?"

As this was the era before cell phones, I flew to the nearest pay phone with a bag of quarters. I called one friend and then another and just kept getting answering machines. Nobody was home. It was a weekday afternoon, so the reason wasn't mysterious. But I was so excited and so eager to share my wild, good news that it was disappointing.

I realized it wasn't too early to call my dad, a professional actor who lived in Los Angeles. I hesitated briefly. The truth was, he had a long history of not being supportive. But he was my dad, and my craving to celebrate this accomplishment overruled my apprehensions. He didn't even know I'd been working on this script, so maybe he would get swept up in this wonderful surprise. Also, it was highly possible his answering machine would pick up, in which case I would just leave a message saying hello. I dialed him. He answered the phone.

I said, "Hey Dad, guess what? I registered my script at the Writers Guild, and —"

Dad immediately interrupted, "Oh no, you're not going to tell me the plot, are you?"

The force of his disregard pierced me like a bullet to the gut. I literally couldn't breathe. The only other time I'd ever had the wind knocked out of me was in second grade, when I was jumping from chair to chair, slipped, and fell so hard that the top rail of the chair went up under my rib cage.

As happens in many crashes and wrecks, time seemed to stand still. Holding the phone, I slumped against the wall of the phone booth. A numbness spread through me as thoughts and images flowed (yes, a disassociated self). A part of me felt like dying. Another part felt already dead. Another part reprimanded me for calling my dad in the first place, as I already knew I couldn't depend on him for support. A wounded little girl inside me was still looking for his love and attention — especially in his chosen field of show business.

"What's going on?" he asked crabbily.

I couldn't speak. I tried. I literally could not take in oxygen, and my lack of breath increased my panic. Simultaneously, a calm and practical part of me reminded me that our bodies have wisdom and, if worse came to worst, I would faint. And that would be good, as I'd automatically start to breathe. That wise and pragmatic alter ego silently recommended that I bend my knees to get closer to the ground and reduce the potential for injuries.

"Oh no, I've done it again! I've hurt your feelings. Oh, God." Dad was annoyed.

Still I couldn't speak. I tried.

"Oh God, now I feel guilty. Say something."

I squeaked.

"Oh God, ughhh!" Dad was frustrated.

Finally I was able to gasp, "I'm going to hang up now."

Dad pleaded, "Don't hang up. I feel so guilty. Oh God, I've done it again."

And you know what I did? Like countless times before, like a good parent (or rather, a parentified adult child), I shifted the focus away from myself and comforted him, checked in on how he was doing, and hung up. Then the tears came, and I made no more telephone calls.

I will not go into details of the self-injurious behavior in which I engaged shortly thereafter. Suffice it to say it was part of a pattern of how I handled the shame and grief underneath my distorted loyalty to my father, which bound me to my core negative belief that I had nothing of value to offer. But this all happened before I discovered voice dialogue, so I was unaware of these dynamics at the time. I now know that my self-injury subpersonalities were doing what they could to protect my vulnerability (despite their painful methods).

Within a few days I'd shaken it all off, abandoned "Mudders," and reentered the busy life curated by my resilient, diligent, resourceful, creative primary selves, who were dedicated to building my first seven-eighths and unequipped for my final eighth. I continued to study acting, audition for parts, and perform improvisation. Then I got an invitation that lit my fire. Again. (One of the ways you can identify if you have a final eighth issue is if you keep returning to the same goal.)

One day a friend asked, "Hey Bridgit, a while back, didn't you say you had a script you wrote?"

"Mmmmm, yes…why?"

Unbeknownst to me, a new sensation, called the internet, was evolving. My friend wanted us to use my script and cast of characters to create a show, which I named *Mudders, the First*

Cyber Sit.comedy. My friend, a technical wizard, managed the complex new technology. I wrote, produced, and costarred in the series (playing the mom). It was great fun and garnered a lot of publicity. In this new incarnation, *Mudders* was regularly compared to the only other significant program on the small web, which was an expensively produced soap opera funded by a huge advertising agency.

When *Mudders* stalled several months later, a buddy suggested I pitch it to this ad agency to see if they'd be interested in partnering with me to produce new episodes of the show with higher production values and commercial viability. They already had a technologically sophisticated, creative team producing a different web series. It was a great idea.

I didn't do it, I'm still ashamed to say. I didn't do the final eighth work of making my project viable. I stalled at the once-in-a-lifetime intersection of a revolutionary new technology supporting narrative content, which could have led to a rewarding and lucrative career of performing and writing. I retreated from the final eighth dream created by my imagination and hard work. Although I didn't realize it at the time, a few parts of myself were terrified of being attacked for my creative output, something that had happened throughout my life. Many of my subpersonalities were still looking for love in all the wrong places. I jumped back into the constricting yet familiar arms of my core negative beliefs.

Of course, if I'd gone ahead, *Mudders* might have failed anyway. That's not the point. The point, and the thing that hurts, is that I abandoned myself and my projects. That's why I'm writing this book — so you don't do it to yourself. The world needs your gifts, no matter what you may have been led to believe.

Pressure has benefits. Subterranean forces on carbon eventually form diamonds, and plate tectonics thrusts new land out of the sea. The chafing discomfort of not being able to finish your project can lead to transformational growth. The double bind has a golden shadow. For parentified children, the golden shadow is that they may develop strengths like resilience, organization, foresight, discipline, humor, problem-solving skills, compassion, persistence, diplomacy, and creativity.

Once you recognize how your inner players spar with one another, you can label your double bind for what it is — distorted loyalty to early influencers and their dogma — and not for what it isn't: proof of the accuracy of your *false* core negative belief. As you gain direct access to the natural gifts embedded within your different selves, you're empowered to transform yourself from an unwitting devotee to your core negative belief to an affirming defender of your final eighth.

Sisyphus

In Greek mythology, Sisyphus was a king who, as a punishment in the afterlife, was ordered to roll a huge boulder to the top of a hill. Every time he neared the pinnacle, Sisyphus and the rock rolled back down to the bottom, picking up more dirt along the way. His fate was to repeat this effort for eternity.

What's my point? I have a few. One, the tale of Sisyphus, destined to fail at his task forever, sounds a bit like the final eighth syndrome, doesn't it? Two, unlike Sisyphus, you're not doomed. I'm here to help. And three, Sisyphus did not fail — he was set up to engage in an impossible task. This is what the double bind does. You're not a failure if you can't lift a sky-scraper. You're not a failure if you can't work 100-hour weeks for months on end even though parts of you want to. The double bind blinds you to the fact that failing at an impossible task is not inadequacy. The following exercise can help you become aware of the core negative beliefs and hidden selves that entrap you in that double bind.

THE FINAL EIGHTH PROCESS
Show Your Double Bind in Action

This exercise involves drawing, but absolutely no skill is required. Stick figures are fine. Switching modes of exploration — engaging a different part of the brain by using pictures and not just words — can be revealing. Use a pencil, pen, crayon, magic marker, paints, charcoal, lipstick, or whatever you like.

Sketch Some Moments

Divide a piece of paper into four boxes by folding or drawing lines. In each box, sketch a distinct moment in a situation in which you found yourself blocked. This is like taking a still photograph of yourself. The image can be related to your final eighth project or some other circumstance where you were locked in an impasse. It doesn't have to be a big, dramatic moment in your life.

You can depict four separate events, or four moments in one event.

Here's an example for guidance. Zoe is a thirty-three-year-old mathematician in a biochemical firm whose final eighth goal was to find a life partner. This was a double bind because finding someone to love, and to love her, was at odds with her core negative belief, "I'm unlovable." She chose to draw four moments surrounding an invitation to tea by someone she liked: Matt, a man she had met at a work event who happened to live nearby.

In the first box, Zoe drew herself with her hand frozen in midair, unable to knock on Matt's door. She felt too shy and scared.

In the second box, she was running to her car in shame.

In the third box, she was in her car, weeping and berating herself as a coward.

The fourth box showed her later that night zoning out at the dinner table with her bickering parents, with whom she lived, pretending she was fine.

Reviewing the exercise, Zoe brought up a point that applies to many people who do this exercise. "Maybe one of the reasons this is so challenging is that, honestly, I could have drawn so many moments like these, representing the same double bind operating in different circumstances throughout my whole life. I could sketch the time I was silent when my mother hurt me by criticizing this amazing outfit I loved. I did not go out that New Year's Eve, despite having three party invitations. I loyally stayed at home so that my parents and I could, once again, share an unpleasant time together. Or the time I turned down a guy who asked me to dance at a reggae festival. Why did I do that? Because he was too handsome!"

Review Your Drawings

Review your drawings and write down which alter egos were involved in the scenarios and their relationship to your core negative belief and your final eighth project.

Zoe realized that each picture reflected her core negative belief that she was unlovable, being acted out by various subpersonalities.

In the first box, her Shy and Scared personas dominated, as they were too scared to let her test whether she was lovable.

In the second box, her Runner and her Cowardly and Ashamed selves prevailed.

In the third box, her Sad Sally and her Inner Critic triumphed.

In the fourth box, Zoe identified "an Underachiever Who Still Lives with Her Parents, plus a disconnected self I call ZoeZombie. And an even deeper self, a very Lonely Soul self, that can be quietly there whether or not other people are around. I guess all of them feel like I can't have the loving life I want."

List the Selves

List three to five selves, primary or hidden, that support your core negative belief (and work against your final eighth goal).

List three to five selves, primary or hidden, that support your final eighth goal.

These lists represent subpersonalities caught in an excruciating tug-of-war, maintaining the double bind between your final eighth and your core negative belief.

Now draw a tug-of-war similar to the illustration below, with one side consisting of each self that is devoted to your core negative belief and the other side consisting of each self that is devoted to your final eighth project.

Core negative belief versus final eighth goal.

Creating this image places you outside yourself, observing your internal gridlock for the first time. Write down any observations you have as you look at your double bind. Take your time.

Get Going — or Let Go?!

True to oneself! Which self? Which of my many…selves?

— KATHERINE MANSFIELD,
The Katherine Mansfield Notebooks

Hanging on to the pain of your disillusion might be serving as protection against the agony of your delusion.

You assume you want the big mansion, the big (hybrid) car, the big bucks, the ambitious career, stardom, the fancy clothes, exotic travel, and the happy-ever-after life with your soulmate (when the polyamorous era ends). Parts of yourself definitely want this — and other parts do not! Perhaps they want to remain hidden, relaxed, and serene. Their desires are jeopardized by goal consummation (whether it's marriage or a raise). There are great reasons to not be totally on board with the big plan. Often, it's not self-sabotage but a form of wise self-protection that's bringing you to a screeching halt.

Now that you have a sense of how different parts of you may be locked in a tug-of-war between your final eighth goal and your core negative beliefs, you may come to a potentially unsettling realization: you may determine that it's time to let go of your goal. Not every plan is consummated, nor should it be. Sometimes not achieving the final eighth is a signal to relinquish the goal. As you free yourself from your double bind and continue to gain clarity and strength, you have permission to drop the ball and walk away from the game. Call it quits. Say goodbye. Throw in the towel. Throw it in the garbage. If you don't want to be here, you're free to go. Free!

There are legitimate reasons for not completing the final eighth. For every gain, there is a loss. Some personas worry that too much change in the status quo will obliterate them. Many subpersonalities enjoy privacy, anonymity, downtime, and low expectations. To these selves, capitalizing on opportunity is a nightmare of being on call and obligated to constantly achieve a new personal best. They prefer to avoid commitment, public exposure, strong emotions, dependence, independence, and change. For some, the mere sensation of acknowledging a need elicits anxiety. Other subpersonalities fear disappointment if their hopes are raised. As you learn the true motivations of your alter egos, you're able to make better-informed decisions.

Maybe you're not moving forward because your goals were imposed on you by family and friends. Is the project really *your* idea? Is it an ambition left over from when you were four, which, let's be honest, doesn't fit anymore? Sometimes a project only *feels* unfinished: it's actually complete, because it has already served its purpose. For example, if after an intense period of emotional writing, you find yourself uninterested in completing your memoir, maybe its true purpose was to be a vehicle for processing and healing your trauma, not a published book.

Are Your Dreams Really Yours?

Simon wanted to discover what was getting in the way of his pursuing venues for exhibiting his art. His apartment was full of his distinctive, witty miniature paintings. Despite living in a metropolitan area with plenty of opportunities to show his art commercially, he rarely followed through. Simon was able to pay his bills by working part time for a nationwide company. The rest of the time he spent in his personal nirvana with colors and brushes.

A part of him felt blessed with his artistic gift. Another part felt guilty, believing he had a moral obligation to do more with his God-given talent. Guilt led to long-term, chronic insomnia. Ironically, the way he dealt with it — by getting out of bed and painting — made his artwork better and better. He sold his signature pieces to family, friends, friends of friends, and family of friends of friends, creating quite a flock of ardent fans. Some of these well-meaning chums went to great lengths to interest gallery owners in his work, sometimes without even telling him. When Simon tried to follow up on these overtures, he invariably bungled things and ended up feeling bad.

Simon determined that his core negative belief was "I'm bad," a vestige of early exposure to a religion he no longer practiced. He also saw that his painting reflected core positive aspects that he hadn't acknowledged: "I am strong, dedicated, persistent, good at concentrating, able to enter a flow state."

His perspective shifted dramatically after he communicated with a variety of his personas. Some of the selves who
supported his thwarted final eighth goal included his Judge-
From-On-High and the Sinner. He was shocked to discover
that they pronounced Simon guilty of a cardinal sin — laziness
— for not pursuing an art career.

His Inner Resistance quickly countered that accusation
with a vital and astonishing insight. The truth was that Simon's
ambitions were no greater than his miniature paintings. He
realized he wasn't stuck: rather, he truly had no aspiration to
market himself and his paintings.

Simon decided to let go of the goal of breaking into the art
scene. He worked on explaining to his friends that although
he appreciated their enthusiasm for his work, their plan for
his future wasn't *his* plan. He followed his deepest desire — to
spend as much time as possible with his canvases.

Put the Old Goal out to Pasture

Here's a really tough question: Is it too late to achieve your
goal? It's worth asking. Reality matters, and time marches on.
You may be a great runner but no longer in contention for
Olympic competition. You may no longer be able to have bi-
ological children. If you're older than a tween, you can't real-
istically hope to become a *professional* ballerina if you haven't
started yet. It's never too late to start dancing (for pleasure or
ballroom competitions) or go to college, but it may be too late
to become a dermatologist. Perhaps your on-again, off-again
lover of many years has married someone else and is reject-
ing invitations to return to your bed. This success interruptus

might be a signal of what your friends are already telling you: Move on! Dealing directly with the issue may cause you hurt now but will help you heal sooner.

Sadly, it's not easy to know when it's time to leave and when to hang on. But boredom and constant lack of motivation may be signs that it's time to let go of a goal. However, the only certainty is uncertainty. So if you leave your project and it comes back to court you again and again, consider reconciliation. Maybe the approach you learn here will help you understand why you stumbled during previous attempts and negotiate a better deal with your various selves this time around: more project and less agony.

One practical reason for failing to complete projects is simply having too many. If that's your struggle, focus on one (or two at most). Put the others in the "Later" file, and if later comes, pick one to concentrate on. Imagine a still photographer trying to decide what to shoot. At some point she has to stop waving her camera around and focus on one thing. The exercises below help explore whether a project should stay or go. Relinquishing old dreams frees up energy to use in other ways. It happens in nature all the time. Snakes and salamanders shed their skins and slither into the new. You can too.

THE FINAL EIGHTH PROCESS
Let Go of a Goal That No Longer Fits

---

1. Imagine what your life would look like if you let go of your final eighth project. Journal what might happen if you walk away from it.

- In what ways will you feel bad?
- In what ways will you feel good?
- Which alter egos will be reassured if you decide this isn't the right goal for you, and why?
- Which ones will feel disappointed or unfulfilled? What do you imagine the people close to you will think — your partner, family, friends, and colleagues?
- Sometimes walking away from a project involves serious consequences. Depending on the situation, who might be good advisers to help you exit ethically and gracefully — mentors, lawyers, therapists, accountants, coaches?
- If you walk away from your goal, what might you aspire to next? Is there anything this goal is keeping you from doing or feeling?

    This exploration will either reignite your desire to continue (I would miss my project, and I don't even know why I was thinking it was a pain in the ass!) or bring relief and certainty that the right thing to do is say goodbye (Wow, if I let it go, I could go hiking every weekend).

2. List positive traits that you've developed as a result of the struggle between your core negative beliefs and your final eighth goal. These qualities are yours to keep, whether or not you complete the goal.

3. Now imagine what your life will look like if you continue to work toward the goal. List the potential costs of success. For example, you may lose privacy, safety, sobriety, superiority, quiet Sunday mornings, or friends. If you can't think of any costs, that's okay. Keep going.

From Impasse to Kickass

And the golden bees
were making white combs
and sweet honey
from my old failures.

— Antonio Machado, "Last Night as I Was Sleeping,"
translated by Robert Bly

The final eighth process detoxes your life and re-
stores energy that you can devote to your project.

At this point in your process you may feel less stuck, but perhaps you're still a bit sticky. What other concerns seem to
take priority over your final eighth completion? In this chapter
we look at some common enticements and distractions and
ways to avoid them.

Substances

Allegiance to counterproductive altered states activated by ex-
cessive drinking or smoking can be hard to give up. Dependence

on substances makes you untrustworthy (to yourself, your circle, your promises, and certainly to your final eighth goal). There's help available to break up with addiction, whether it's to pills, poker, porn, or anything else that compulsively calls you away from yourself for hours and hours. One client had an inner self that admitted to being part of the force immobilizing her. This subpersonality reported, "Until she gets her drinking under control, there's no chance of flowering." This wasn't a punitive Inner Critic: it was a persona offering an accurate assessment of her troubles in vital domains of her life, including her physical and financial well-being. If you have problems with addiction, find help to get it under control. That may be your most vital final eighth goal.

Your Brain on Ideas

There is a less obvious altered state that has the same effect as addictive substances: inaction. Beware the danger of the high of unlimited possibility and endless potential, of which you excitedly spill the details to friends (perhaps over drinks: oh, the fun!). When your brain is high on ideas, elation and euphoria can intensify to the point that parts of you actually feel the goal is already accomplished. When the exhilaration wears off, the hangover symptoms may include low motivation, malaise, boredom, fatigue, overwhelm, grogginess, crabbiness, and achiness.

One remedy is to convert this avoidance tactic into action by doing a voice dialogue session with the parts of you who are great at daydreaming and visualizing. Learn what they have to say, and when possible, take concrete steps toward achieving their dreams.

The Mirage Goal

It can be a shock to find that the skills you learned in your family of origin are not what's necessary to succeed in the adult world (say, relying on charm or talent, or always being polite). We want assurance that the rules we were originally taught are valid: that education always leads to opportunity, that obeying the rules is rewarded. I have been astonished at the depth of despair and anger clients feel when they realize they need to shift away from their elementary-school success formulas.

A mirage is an optical illusion, something you encounter along your path that appears real, solid, and within reach, but doesn't exist. Sometimes when you're stalled, you increase your level of activity using your customary strategies, which seduces you into thinking you're making progress. Instead of focusing on accessing other parts of yourself and developing new and scary abilities like being assertive and not waiting for permission, you double down on perfecting your routine tactics, like being nicer or not airing your opinions. But this is a distraction that turns your final eighth goal into a mirage goal, perpetuating the double bind.

Working hard matters, but for many determined, diligent people, that is not the issue holding them back. When it hit one of my talented and persevering clients that working harder was not how he was going to succeed at his final eighth goal of landing a television writing gig, he wailed, "It's not fair!"

Yes, it isn't! He had done well in writing contests and regularly gotten positive feedback. But his core negative belief that he wasn't good enough caused him to fear the tasks necessary to achieve his final eighth goal: developing alter egos who were good at interpersonal networking, competitive collaboration, and salesmanship. His mentor told him he was hiding in the role of student and not daring to come out as a master of his craft. Even with this insight, he kept working at perfecting his scripts instead of strategically and boldly following up with his contacts. Sadly, this course of action led him to squander rich opportunities. The final eighth truly is an inside job.

The alter egos that entice you to be "productive" (crazy-busyness, perfectionism, overresearching, etc.) or "unproductive" (disorganization, indecision, laziness, euphoria, confusion, free-floating anxiety, if-onlys, and more) are trying to protect you from judgment, good or bad, external or internal. This strategy keeps you in sight of your goal, but prevents you from actually achieving it and exposing your efforts, and yourself, to evaluation by the outside world. Be aware of traps that lead you to pursue your goal but never achieve it.

The Forgiveness Trap

One enterprise that might take a lot of your time (and divert effort away from your final eighth goal) is the pursuit of forgiving those who have hurt you. Perhaps despite your attempts to let go of blame and to grant a pardon, you still find yourself tormented with unbidden thoughts and troublesome emotions. Perhaps while you're brushing your teeth or doing something else that's good for your physical health, you become aware that your mind is festering with recollections of painful events, encounters, missed opportunities, or injustices. Parts of you are seething with rage and socially unacceptable emotions like resentment, hurt, anger, vulnerability, despair, sadness, and vengefulness. And other parts of you are upset by your inability to forgive and forget. You've bought into the positivity movement's pressure to avoid expressing difficult emotions because that will forever trap you in the negativity jail. I disagree.

This was also my dilemma. I wanted to forgive and to be free. I tried. And I tried. And even though I never quite understood what was required in order to forgive, I tried again. It didn't work for me. Over time I realized a few things. One is that you need time to be with, and acknowledge, the pain you've suffered in order to let it go. The parts of yourself that hold painful truths need to be heard and validated and to have their gifts and stings honored. Pressure to forgive can feel like the bad old days when you just shut up. You don't really forgive — you just stop sharing how you feel.

Blameography

I struggled with not being able to forgive for years. Then I had an epiphany when I heard a famous and successful person who built a remarkable and inspirational life against huge odds speak. He described his rough childhood, including going hungry and being beaten by his alcoholic mother. He forgave his mom. I realized that every time he repeats that he forgave his horrific parent, he honors the wounded parts that know the truth of his childhood as well as the resilient, powerful, and wildly creative inner selves that worked to free him.

Toward that end, I suggest a blameography. Acknowledging your pain, resentment, and anger empowers you by releasing their pent-up energy. Expression of these emotions and opinions is often mistaken for having a negative mindset, which means an inability to see anything but the worst, ugliest scenarios. This process is different. It involves acknowledging wounded parts that need validation. Allowing them to be heard is a major thrust of the final eighth process.

THE FINAL EIGHTH PROCESS
A Blameography

A blameography follows the style of a bibliography, which is simply a list of source material. This exercise is a great way to identify the roots of your painful emotions in order to release them. Have fun being mad.

Think of an experience that continues to plague you. Briefly describe it and list your grievances.

Here are a few of my examples:

Dad, My. You chose your addictions over me. I blame you for making me think I was a burden who shouldn't live.

Halloween Day Parade. NYC, 1989. Too many people, including naked partiers hanging off fire escapes — literally crushing me into the wall for a very long time — so now I avoid Mardis Gras, raves, and penny socials.

Smith, Martin. Psychology professor, freshman year in college. You spoke in an endless monotone, boring me away from my passion for years and years.

If you're crying in protest, "Isn't this focusing on the negative? Why do this?" — well, then *don't* do this. Work on your final eighth project instead. But if you're immobilized, a blameography might be just the thing. This exercise helps identify and release deep emotional blocks that may be helping maintain your double bind. Paradoxically, engaging in this somewhat taboo exercise might actually ease you into gratitude for gifts that came out of your misfortune. Lurking close behind might be genuine forgiveness.

Poisoned Assets

In childhood, when one of our attributes is invalidated, we may unconsciously develop a negative relationship with it. This is similar to the covert way core negative beliefs make people feel bad. My client Rhonda had a perfect example. As a kid she loved swinging high on her favorite swing. When her mother abruptly pulled her off the swing seat to leave the playground, Rhonda became cranky and stomped her feet. Her mother snarled, "I look forward to the day you have children — you'll see what suffering feels like!" Growing up with this refrain, hearing her mom repeat that she looked forward to seeing her suffer, poisoned Rhonda's spontaneity, joy, and ability to be in the flow.

The situation was simple. One person wanted to stay at the playground longer, and the other person, who held total control, had a different agenda. But instead of being aware of these power dynamics and helping her daughter shift from the fun of the swing to the disappointment of having to leave, the mother threw a painful curse at her daughter. And it happened often. Rhonda couldn't articulate it at the time, but she viscerally understood she was dependent on someone who considered her a burden.

Rhonda internalized that message into "I'm bad." Some of the primary selves who tried to help her cope were High Anxiety, the Accommodator, the Ordinary, the Sad One, Miz Responsibility, and the Procrastinator. When, as an adult, she was trying to conceive a child, she realized she was stalled in her final eighth largely because a very young part of her was terrified she would be trapped into a miserable adulthood. Her final eighth process helped her uncover her hidden Optimist, Adventurer, Healer, Tender One, and Visionary (who repeatedly reminded Rhonda that there are always better options available than her mother's curse). She also dialogued with her Playful Child and in the process, retrieved her spontaneity and joy.

Another style of asset poisoning is growing up with back-handed compliments — insults disguised as praise. An example? "For you, that was brave" is a contemptuous observation that implies cowardice, despite your having taken an action that took courage. Another example might be, "Way to go! I never expected you to get that promotion," insinuating your inherent inferiority and ineligibility. Have you experienced similar demeaning endorsements?

Another way your good qualities might have been undermined is by direct attack:

- Your strength: maybe you were accused of being intimidating or competitive ("which is ugly") and threatened with rejection and abandonment.
- Your creativity: maybe you were accused of being flighty, inconsequential, or weird, or demeaned as stupid for not doing things the "right" way.
- Your confidence: maybe you were accused of being arrogant, bossy, or aggressive; maybe you were ridiculed as a know-it-all when you got an answer right; or when you got something wrong, maybe you were ridiculed as deluded for thinking you knew the answer.

Perhaps you don't have any poisoned assets. But before reaching that conclusion, consider in which areas in your life you feel free to be yourself. For example, you may enjoy planning travel and enjoying regular trips, even if you don't always have the budget for your dream vacation. However, if a part of you really wants to travel but something always interferes with a trip, this might be a final eighth conflict. If you never seem to take that trip to your ancestral land, your adventurousness and imagination might be poisoned assets. Are you hanging on to guilt for leaving, for having fun, for not suffering?

Hunger indicates desire: it informs you that you want something, which ideally motivates you to forage for something nurturing. You may be stuck because your appetite was criticized or curbed in the past (perhaps you were called greedy or selfish), and now you are unconsciously restricting access to the hungry parts of yourself that can help get you across the finish line. Does that mean you are fated for starvation and stuckness in the final eighth? (Hint: no.) The final eighth process facilitates a direct, healthy relationship with your assets. Side effects might include joy, hope, giddiness, and the urge to get a Hula-Hoop. As with any detox program, it might feel a little destabilizing to have access to your pure, uncontaminated version of that asset, whether it's charisma, appetite, or love.

THE FINAL EIGHTH PROCESS
Detox Your Assets

In this exercise you'll draw two different spider graphs, sometimes called radial graphs.

1. In the center of a piece of paper, draw a circle — about an inch and a half across. Inside the circle, write the name of one of your poisoned assets.

Surround this with three circles that connect to the center circle. In each one, write one way in which that asset was put down or poisoned.

2. In the center of another piece of paper, draw another circle of the same size. Inside the circle, write the name of the same asset. Surround this with three circles that connect to the center circle. In each one, write the name of an alter ego that can now positively channel this asset.

The illustration shows the spider graphs from Rhonda, who chose joy as her poisoned asset.

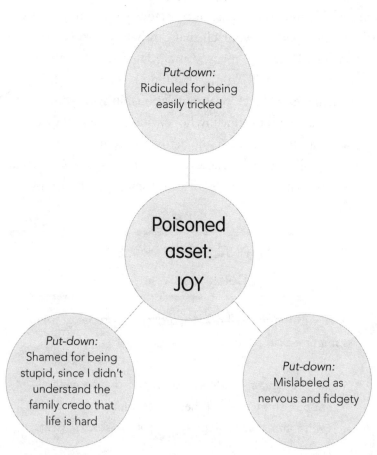

Put-down:
Ridiculed for being easily tricked

Poisoned asset:
JOY

Put-down:
Shamed for being stupid, since I didn't understand the family credo that life is hard

Put-down:
Mislabeled as nervous and fidgety

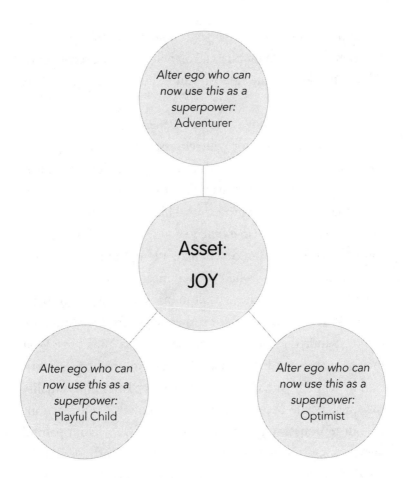

Turn Envy into Your Magic Wand

We've all had attacks of envy and resentment. When you feel a stab of envy, you automatically conclude that the target of your envy has what you covet because they're superior. This implicitly classifies you as inferior, someone who will never have the qualities it takes to acquire your desire. This fuels your core negative belief, as you seethe in any combination of stomach-churning, muscle-clenching, burning shame, inadequacy, deprivation, and self-loathing.

Completion of your final eighth goal may lead you from experiencing envy to inciting it. You will discover a secret: both sides of the coin of envy are painful! It hurts to envy as well as to be envied.

Let's break this down. At its root, envy is a system alerting you that you want for yourself assets that another person seems to have through their advantages, possessions, attitudes, and successes. Envy makes us vulnerable, and our inner selves respond instinctively to protect us. This often means that varying alter egos mobilize in a frenzy of judgment against the person we envy. We put her down in an attempt to feel better. We label her negatively — whatever that means for us. We may call the person we envy a know-it-all, an undeserving jerk, or privileged. When we feel envy for someone we greatly admire, we may conclude that we can never measure up. Your Lone Wolf may help you avoid the person because you feel so insignificant in her company. Or your Number One Fan subpersonality may push you to become her devoted follower. These reactions are our responses to the qualities of people who, in our painful view, belong to a club we can never get into. Shrouded in the discontent, desire, awe, resentment, and dislike we feel toward the people we envy is also envy of the permission they give themselves to reap the benefits of their assets, assets that may have been poisoned for us.

Are you ready to hear another vital secret? The people you envy often lead with *your* hidden selves. As painful as the lessons may feel, these mortals are your teachers. They represent what Carl Jung calls your golden shadow, your hidden creative potential.

Instead of cringing in agony, consider envy as a magic

wand illuminating parts of yourself that need to be embraced in order for you to complete your final eighth. Hal and Sidra Stone created a remedy that transforms envy into energy that you can use immediately to empower yourself. It's founded on the principle of homeopathy, that like cures like. Ailments are treated with tiny, diluted doses of the substance that in full strength causes the excruciating symptoms. The exercise below shows you how to bestow some of your alter egos with superpowers by taking in a teeny amount of the quality that incites envy.

THE FINAL EIGHTH PROCESS
From Envy to Eminence

List two people you envy, or admire to such a degree you feel you will never measure up. For each, list two specific traits that incite envy in you.

Pick one of these people and a single trait that you envy. It might be someone who's so popular that your envy leads you to judge them as a shallow exhibitionist, or someone who's so smart you're in awe.

The remedy is to ask yourself: If I take a diluted teeny-weeny, itty-bitty, micro-mini dose of this trait, how might I behave differently? Write down your response.

Sharon, a workshop participant, gave this example: "I negatively judge my colleague as arrogant. But what if I had access to a microdose of my own arrogance? I would have a right-sized sense of my worth, which would make me more genuinely confident."

Having identified the remedy, what will you do differently within the next three days?

Sharon wrote, "Having taken my microdose of arrogance, I will call my supervisor now and let her know I'm not available to work weekends this month. She will have to find someone else. Because I really am that fabulous!"

Repeat with another quality, as necessary.

Who's the Boss of Me?

Reassign Roles and Raise New Selves

It takes a long time to get to be a diva. I mean, you gotta work at it.

— DIANA ROSS

Divas and wild ones come in all forms and fashions.

Dialoguing with your inner selves creates a new habit of innovative attention that breaks automatic responses, quiets overly dominant inner selves, and leads you to consider alternatives that would never have otherwise occurred to you.

You can't break up with subpersonalities. They're part of you forever. But in this chapter you'll learn how to give your personas updated roles when their original functions, including supporting your negative beliefs and keeping you knotted in your double bind, are no longer wanted. For example, the toxic Inner Critic who left you too demoralized to progress can

121

be repurposed into a canny ally able to see the difference between great opportunities and dead-end moves.

We'll also look at ways to connect or reconnect with ener-
gized, resilient, strong parts of yourself that can help you cross
your finish line. Some of these may be long-hidden selves, but
others might be completely new to you: an Inner Wild One, a
Diva, a Problem Solver, a Choreographer, or a Fierce Competitor who likes a challenge.

Repurposing Your Inner Critic

The Inner Critic is programmed to be suspicious of anything
new. It is wired toward attachment to your early caregivers and
their core negative beliefs. To this persona, the final eighth is
perilous! Because its honorable task is to protect you by avoid-
ing abandonment, it's hypervigilant for dangers like judgment,
hurt, shame, or rejection. Its dysfunctional strategy is to criti-
cize you before someone else does in the hopes of making you
"better" in some way. Your Inner Critic simultaneously assumes you're inferior (which effectively enforces core negative
beliefs) and urges you to move ahead (which presupposes that
you have the ability to do so) and thus berates you both for
being inferior and for squandering your superior talents. This
keeps you in your double bind, a dynamic your Inner Critic
may not have been aware of until now.

Who does your Inner Critic work for? Think about that for
a minute. Does your Inner Critic work for you? I don't think so.
Otherwise it would obey when you give it an order. Your Inner
Critic works for your early caregivers and perhaps some of the
folks referenced in your blameography. Out of this instinctive

devotion, the Inner Critic can behave like a bully who resorts to threats and stalking. Making you feel bad keeps you in your double bind. It makes you the servant of your Inner Critic and core negative beliefs, holding you back from your final eighth.

The Inner Critic's gifts are that it never seems to run out of energy or creativity, second-guess itself, or become overwhelmed with insecurity. Hal and Sidra Stone describe the Inner Critic as having "the intelligence of a genius, an uncanny intuition, an ability to analyze our feelings and motivations, a sweeping gaze that notices the tiniest of details, and, in general, an unerring ability to see and to magnify all our faults and shortcomings. It seems to be a lot more intelligent and perceptive than we ordinary mortals are."

The energy and insights of the Inner Critic are like fire, which can either be harnessed to sauté piquant truffle fries or let loose to burn the barn down. Here's an exercise that can help harness the skills of your Inner Critic and other parts.

THE FINAL EIGHTH PROCESS
Promote Your Alter Egos

List Abilities of Inner Critic

List some abilities of your Inner Critic. Feel free to use your gift and sting lists from the exercises in chapters 2 and 4, if you've made them for this alter ego.

As an example, here are my Inner Critic's abilities:

- The ability to keenly observe how I don't measure up.
- The ability to brutally assess how I don't measure up.
- Limitless energy to judge how I don't measure up.

Surprise your Inner Critic with a love letter. Thank it for having been such a loyal protector, with its blind devotion to saving you from abandonment at any cost. Let it know that the days of living as if your core negative beliefs were true are over. It is now the era of core positivity. In a word or two, describe how that feels. Some of my clients have chosen words such as *radiant, free,* and *liberated.*

Redefine and upgrade the talents and creative energies of the Inner Critic for beneficial use. Its laser-sharp perception is now assigned to supporting your final eighth goals.

Here's how my Inner Critic's abilities are reassigned:

- Its ability for keen observation can be applied to polishing my writing.
- Its ability for brutal assessment can be transformed into highly efficient time management, reminding me that if I want to accomplish all I hope to in a day, I need to get organized first.
- Its limitless energy to judge can be transformed into a vast supply of energy to fuel my creativity and fun curiosity instead of reinforcing my core negative belief.

List Abilities of Another Subpersonality

List some abilities of another subpersonality. Feel free to use your gift and sting list, if you've made one for this alter ego.

Here are examples from a client who recommissioned her Perfectionist:

- Ability to maintain high standards, which I never measure up to.
- Ability to be tireless, which makes me feel terrible, as, inevitably, I don't measure up.
- Ability to be competitive, though I never measure up or make the cut.

Again, surprise this alter ego with a love letter thanking it for its protection and letting it know that the time of living as if your core negative beliefs were true is over. It is now the era of core positivity. In a word or two, describe how that feels.

Promote Other Selves

Reassign and promote the talents and creative energies of these other selves. Make sure you assign them roles appropriate to their age and strengths: in other words, don't ask your Magical Inner Child to function as the CEO of your final eighth project.

Here's how my client reassigned the superpowers of her Perfectionist:

- The Perfectionist's high standards will be applied to make my home beautiful, because it makes me feel good and I deserve it.
- The ability to be tireless will be applied to my final eighth goal, without my core negative belief putting the brakes on me all the time.
- Its competitiveness will be assigned to motivating me so that when I set out to do something, like my final eighth, I have the strength to persevere.

Enter the Diva

Where does the Diva come in? Stage left, of course, with musical accompaniment! The Inner Diva is a fabulous part of yourself that is entitled and sassy and intends to get her needs met. Obviously, a Diva comes in many or any wonderful genders, but I'm asserting the author's privilege and using *she*. The Diva prioritizes her needs and wants. She's strong and not shy about believing in herself, and she doesn't wait for approval from the outside world to embark on her final eighth adventure.

A Diva's point of view is, "Hey, you never know. A misstep can slip, slide, and syncopate into some kickin' choreography!"

One of my favorite overheard conversations was between two women who ran into each other on a subway train. As her friend scooted over next to her, the seated woman said, "Hi! You look great."

The other woman appeared surprised, even shocked. There was a pause as they looked at each other.

Then she replied, "Of course."

She was not being snotty. Her philosophy was obviously "I am. Therefore, I am fabulous." They both smiled and started to catch up.

If you aren't happy with an Inner Diva, you might prefer an Inner Daredevil, or any other persona with bold, forward-motion energy. Another wonderful persona is the Wild One, a passionate self who leads with the heart, doesn't want to be forced into a box, and isn't afraid of making mistakes. This fearlessness is vital for navigating the uncharted territory of the final eighth. For many, this bold persona is a hidden self, which you may have come to know through your poisoned assets detox or by taking a teeny dose of a characteristic you envy.

As always, go back to basics and have a voice dialogue session to find out more about this self (see chapter 3). The voice dialogue process is helpful to return to, especially when a self seems mystifying.

If you have no connection to your Inner Diva, Daredevil, or Wild One, your Inner Critic won't obey your cease-and-desist notice. You will stay in thrall to your core negative beliefs, locked in your double bind. You may find it impossible to move forward without someone giving you permission first. But in the final eighth territory, there are no permission slips. Entering this territory means defending yourself and your style, taking yourself seriously, and unknotting your double bind. Take center stage. Find your light. Shine, baby, shine!

Breaking Up Isn't Necessarily Hard to Do

My friend was sad that she had not yet met her life partner, and she made that her final eighth goal. She committed to actively dating, which was not always easy. She went through the final eighth process, became aware of many of her selves, and identified her core negative belief as "I'm broken." When she found her Inner Diva, much to her surprise and mine, she discovered she relished unleashing this persona. When it was clear someone she was dating was not a final eighth contender, she would saunter to her soon-to-be ex's workplace, express genuine appreciation for their connection, and graciously break up over a casual lunch.

She said, "Who knew? I love breaking up! Ghosting is for cowards."

She felt that having the courage to break up gave her clarity and energy to keep going. "When I let go, even though it might be painful, I'm able to see what I really have and assess what isn't right. And that's empowering." (In case you're wondering, she is now happily married.)

Breaking up can be hard to do, but keep an open mind. Be curious. You might be wrong in ways that please you. While you're at it, don't forget to break up with your core negative beliefs and with any false standards of flawlessness. The final eighth process is not about being perfect. Even breaking up doesn't always go perfectly: sometimes we make up after a breakup, and then we have to break up again! Maybe it's time to break up with your pessimism, skepticism, and self-criticism, or abandon your lackadaisical attitude.

Imagine walking around, present to every moment, with direct access to the magnificence of your Inner Diva, Daredevil, or Wild One, while still under the healthy guardianship of your Inner Critic (who knows you're the boss)! That's the freedom these exercises lead you to.

THE FINAL EIGHTH PROCESS
Access Potent Selves

If you need help getting to know your Inner Diva, Daredevil, or Wild One, here are some fun ways to do it.

Write down three instances when you behaved like a Diva or Daredevil.

Think of three Divas, Daredevils, or Wild Ones you either know personally or know of.

Do an inner voice dialogue session with your Inner Diva, Daredevil, or Wild One. Here are a few questions to ask:

- Who are you? Do you have a name?
- What role or function do you serve in [your name]'s life?
- What rule, or rules, do you think [your name] needs to obey in order to be successful?
- Are you in a particular part of [your name]'s body?
- What is your energy like? Loose, constricted, wide open, lethargic, frenetic, mellow?
- How do you know what you know?
- How do you dress for success?

If you find yourself slipping into dysfunctional loyalty to your core negative belief and Inner Critic, conjure the energy of your Inner Diva, Daredevil, or Wild One by listening to great music, wearing amazing shoes, or recalling a sensuous memory of a time when you were rockin'. Embody that part and take some final eighth steps.

CHAPTER

11 Cross Your Finish Line

A celebration to last throughout the years,
So bring your good times, and your laughter too.

— KOOL & THE GANG, "Celebration"

Crossing the finish line unleashes many emotions.
Some are huge, wild waves of elation. Others are
wisps of ecstasy and quiet gratitude.

The final eighth process helps you see and activate your potential and make choices that are in tune with your deepest desires. You now have a much greater sense of who you are. By exploring your subpersonalities, identifying your core negative beliefs and your double bind, extricating yourself from their paralyzing forces, reassigning some of your alter egos, and encountering hidden personas, you move into final eighth territory. This is nothing short of metamorphosis, the emergence of your new identity.

The painful obstacles to completing your project have led you on this amazing journey of discovering that your embodied identities inadequately expressed your essential being. The struggle is part of the transformational process. What would happen if you helped a new butterfly get out of its cocoon by carefully cutting it out? It would die, because you would have robbed it of the challenges that develop the strength it needs to break free, leave the chrysalis, and fly into life.

Shake Your New Tale

Kerry kept getting close to fulfilling his final eighth dream — working in Africa or the Middle East with a nongovernmental organization that aids refugees. But something always shoved him off course at the last minute. He went through the final eighth process and met some alter egos he liked and some he didn't: his Enthusiast (an energetic part that fizzled quickly), his Panicker (who, he discovered, wasn't worried about the dangers of working in war zones but was terrified something would happen to his mother while he was gone), his I-Can't-Possibly (an unconfident self), and the subpersonality he called the Cork ("It holds in my effervescence and makes sure I don't make trouble"). Through the Cork, he uncovered his core negative belief: "I'm too much trouble." He came to understand that the alter egos who opposed his goal bought into that belief. Working abroad would cause too much trouble for his mother, his siblings, his partner, and his current employer. The rule he followed that kept him bound in inaction and faithful to his core negative belief was "Don't rock the boat!"

Through the final eighth process, Kerry met a hidden sub-personality he chose to nurture: the Captain of the Ship. This persona helped Kerry to get his team of selves working toward his goal and to land the job he wanted. He was set to sail to Syria!

Then backsliding ensued, with a resurgence of fears and almost crippling guilt when his mom didn't share his joy at his good news and actively discouraged him from going. Kerry relapsed into a flood of second thoughts. But he continued his voice dialogue sessions to connect to what really resonated with him. Today, he's living his final eighth as he supports Syrian refugees with a nonprofit organization closer to home — and feels that all his selves are just where they're supposed to be.

THE FINAL EIGHTH PROCESS
Cross Your Finish Line!

You're plugged into your correct power source — your liberated truth. Relish your new relationship with your uniqueness. Enjoy brimming energy as you tap into the resources of your limitless, creative, courageous selves. Now that you have access to your multiple styles of wisdom, you are free to cross your finish line. Congratulations!

CHAPTER

12 Practice Safe Success

Strangely, times of success are most dangerous for me.

— MIKE TYSON

Practicing safe success means protecting yourself by matching the right alter ego and the right superpower to the occasion. Sometimes you need your Lover, and sometimes you need your Lawyer!

Crossing your finish line can be a time of joyful celebration. But that can be followed by a myriad emotions that might include melancholy as well as pride and joy. The final eighth is not the end: the cycle starts anew. As you arrive at your finish line, new destinations beckon. Completing the final eighth is almost guaranteed to bring you back to a first eighth. If you've

135

won an Olympic medal, do you try to make the team again —
or do you do something completely different?

Think about what you'd like to do next. One talented performer created her own show with a large cast, which got rave
reviews. When the show ended, she went into a period of despair because she missed it all so much. This melancholy made
her desperate and clouded her ability to choose her next project, until her Wisdom alter ego recommended she take a step
back. You too have that hard-earned acumen at your disposal.

Once you've achieved a final eighth goal, you are different,
and different rules apply. Going from "I coulda been a contender" to "I'm a winner" can feel like sailing into a magnificent sunset. But in real life, that's not the end of the story. What
happens when the dawn arrives? The new seas you're cruising
in may not always be smooth. To adjust to the often disorienting reality of achieving your dream, you need to practice what
I call safe success.

Now that you're no longer working against yourself, you
can make better use of many of the wonderful productivity
tools and methods that are out there, strategies you may have
technically used correctly in the past, but which did not lead
to success: action plans, business plans, five-year plans, and
personal financial plans. Now that you know which subpersonalities are involved, you'll be able to make more thought-
ful choices. If the tool works, use it. But make sure it's in the
hands of the right subpersonality, which will bestow such
techniques with superpowers. A classic example would be
doing research for your dissertation, which reflects a remarkable seven-eighths' worth of accomplishments. However, if
this vital component of your PhD is put in the hands of your

Perfectionist, Critic, Procrastinator, Good Girl/Boy, Restless Intellectual, Visionary, Scared of Applying for Academic Positions, Scared of Academic Committees and Department Heads, or Scared of Intimacy alter egos, you risk being trapped on a treadmill of never-ending research, never making the shift from research to writing your dissertation. This turns finishing your research into a mirage goal. If, instead, you put your research into the hands of the appropriate subpersonalities (perhaps your Focuser, Project Manager, Strategizer, or Realist), you will end up with a well-documented dissertation. In order to complete it, try calling in some Finish Line selves, like your Inner Editor, Academic, and Expert.

Extinction Bursts

What makes you strong can also make you vulnerable. The misperception is that as we grow more robust, wiser, and more aware we need less protection. In fact, we may need more. As you embrace the final eighth process and feel its positive, empowering influence, you may suddenly find yourself backsliding. This is normal.

In behavioral science, *extinction* refers to the gradual fading of particular behaviors. As you get closer to your final eighth goal, the selves who are attached to your core negative belief, including your Inner Critic, may pull out big fat weapons to derail your progress and keep you trapped in your double bind. This is called an *extinction burst*, a sudden and temporary increase in old, self-defeating urges. Even though your Inner Critic may be screaming that you're a loser, this experience means that you're winning. But if you give in to the parts of you that support your core negative belief, you will be at risk of losing.

If you experience these brief, fierce impulses to relapse or fall into old patterns, stick with what you've learned in the final eighth process: pay attention, identify which inner selves are active at any given moment, and understand their competing agendas. You now have the power to choose which alter egos are in control. Congratulations — an extinction burst is a sign you're doing a lot of things right.

Hooray for Feng Shui

Practicing safe success includes using the assets you already have as well as strengthening parts of yourself, growing new parts, and tolerating the distress of throwing away what no longer fits (like core negative beliefs and that raggedy shirt). Feng shui is the ancient Chinese technique of balancing the energies in your physical space to support health and good fortune, and you can do it with your mental space as well. The final eighth goal of a colleague was to break up with his long-time girlfriend. When they ultimately split up, he found himself soaring with energy that had been tied up in his dilemma. He cleaned house, threw out lots of unnecessary items, and rearranged his furniture. (Notice that none of this takes money.) He followed his impulse to build wall art that became an altar of sensual images celebrating his new bachelor era. Before he even hit the apps, he was dating and having fun, while simultaneously being careful to reserve some alone time so that he could process his new final eighth status and not jump into something that would end up pulling him into old patterns. That's safe success.

Do you have space and time carved out for celebrating your final eighth completion (or honoring your new first eighth)? Your plan might entail doing nothing for the next month and taking a long, long nap every weekend. The physical, material world matters too. Look at your home. Is your environment in disarray? If the stuff around you does not support your expressed goal, what does it support? Your surroundings maintain your status quo. What alter egos are in charge of your space? Do you need to break up with your mess? Do you need to add anything, like a file cabinet or an easel? If you collect magazines for your collages, are they in demoralizing crap piles so that when the urge to create hits, it melts almost simultaneously? The best approach is to take action. Throw the bum out — whether it's a broken toaster, dust bunny, or mooching roommate. Make space for your goal.

Take a Hit of Gratitude

As you struggle with the difficulties inherent in all challenges, pessimism you barely notice may float in and trigger your core negative belief, locking you in your double bind. Maybe it's a wisp of a memory of being disappointed by a friend. This jolt of demoralization triggers a low-grade gloom that saps your desire to stretch yourself. Regular hits of negativity are a mood-altering habit that disables forward motion. If you find you're mindlessly toking on these downers, especially when it's time to work, put them out.

Instead, take a hit of gratitude: revel in the feelings of happiness you have about something wonderful that's already in your life. This can be as simple as savoring the ability to swallow, sharing your bees' honey with the neighbors, or remembering when you won your election. While in this positive mindset, shift your focus to a concrete step you can take toward your goal now.

Safe Success Tracker

We are warned about fair-weather friends, who stick around only during the good times and flee when the going gets rough. Rarely discussed is the pain and heartache caused by foul-weather kin and companions. When some of my clients achieved success in their goals, they were shocked by the negative, unsupportive reactions of people around them. Family and friends who don't want you to succeed are dissatisfied with themselves. Don't make their dissatisfaction yours.

Who do you share your dreams with? How do they react? Be honest. If your friends feed on negativity, get new friends. This ugly phenomenon is deep-rooted and widespread. *Schadenfreude* is the German word for taking pleasure from the misfortunes of others and resonates with most people when they first hear it. How is it we don't have a similar word in English?

You may not get a lot of outside support to help you handle your success. Who do you call when your first book gets the biggest presale offer in the history of the publishing company? That happened to a colleague — who was stunned and distraught when longtime friends actively minimized the significance and value of her triumph. After a short period of resentment and grief, she used the final eighth process and began to access extroverted alter egos and expanded her social circle, which now includes many supportive allies. What do you do when you start to say no to certain people and situations so that you stay true to yourself, and they don't like it?

One way to address the difficulties that arise from success is to create a Safe Success Tracker. Devote a section of your final eighth journal or file, or start a new one, to keep tabs on how you're handling crossing the finish line. Jot down any event, exchange, or emotion that seems to have been triggered by your recent success. Note what action you took (or didn't take). Which self was in charge? Were you pleased with the way you handled things? If not, what might you have done differently? What selves might have helped?

Here are notes from the Safe Success Tracker kept by Wanda, a workshop participant:

> **The exchange:** For years, I've been meeting my friend Gayle every week at a café and basically complaining about our jobs. I thought she'd be happy for me that I'm living my final eighth and now have my dog walking and grooming business. Instead, she's been subtly putting me down. This week she as much as said I was incompetent. I'm sad and mad she was up for coffee and kvetching, but not java and joy.
>
> **The action I took:** I found myself downplaying how much fun I'm having and how proud I am. To stay connected to Gayle, I make myself small and put

myself down so she won't feel bad. I was not at all pleased with the action I took!

What selves were in charge: When I acted like my new business was nothing special, the personas that were in charge were my selves who fear abandonment and wonder if my core negative belief, about not being good enough, is true. I didn't want to upset Gayle. Plus, my Inner Critic reminded me of a small mistake I made last week, and I wondered for a few seconds if Gayle was right that I'm incompetent. That put the brakes on me!

What I could have done differently: I could have gotten in touch with my Inner Diva and confronted Gayle and asked why she's not happier for me. My Inner Diva would tell her, "My life's surrounded by love right now. Between the dogs and their humans, not only do I get paid really well doing something I'd do for free, but I get snuffled and kissed all day!" Also, my Empath, my Impervious-to-Criticism, and my Worker Bee subpersonalities would definitely have been helpful.

Wanda realized her Worker Bee and her Deep Connector kept her business buzzing, and she delighted in the contentment and confidence those superpowers gave her. Armed with her inner allies, Wanda tried many tactics, including diplomatically handling Gayle's envy by understanding that Gayle was scared of abandonment and change. She also summoned the resilience of her Impervious-to-Criticism self to shield herself from Gayle's negativity.

However, none of this prevented Gayle from continuing to

undermine Wanda. Gayle was bound firmly in her own core negative belief and hampered by unacknowledged hidden selves. The information Wanda gained from her Safe Success Tracker convinced her to let the friendship go. She then accomplished another final eighth — letting go of toxic relationships and choosing appropriate mentors, guides, and allies.

THE FINAL EIGHTH PROCESS
Practice Safe Success

1. Start your Safe Success Tracker.
2. As you move through your final eighth and into your first eighth, it's more than likely you'll be stymied by new situations. That's okay — that's living! Note which alter egos step in when efforts are rewarded beyond expectation, and note which ones you might need to access or strengthen when difficulties arise.

As you revel in your final eighth, I invite you to consider the wisdom of the visionary Shakti Gawain from her classic *Creative Visualization*: "This is a time of great transformation on our planet. We all have a part to play, just by being willing to be our true, magnificent selves."

Staying Connected

As you embark on your final eighth odyssey, it's my deepest hope that the material and exercises in this book are helpful and you make major strides toward the goals you've set for yourself. If you have questions, feedback, and/or discoveries during the course of your final eighth process, please feel free to reach out. I'd love to hear how it's going.

My email is final8th@final8th.com

To learn the latest and stay updated on my offerings like workshops, retreats, scheduling sessions, and more, regularly visit my website. I am available for final eighth keynotes, speaking engagements, and trainings.

My website is www.final8th.com

Please stay in touch via social media.

My Instagram is @bridgitdengelgaspard
My Twitter and Facebook are @BridgitGaspard

I look forward to hearing how you're doing on your journey.

Acknowledgments

As I dove into the concept of the final eighth, I began to recognize the truth of Richard Bach's insight "We teach best what we most need to learn." The process of writing this book included wrestling with my own long-standing final eighth issues. Along the way I was supported by a large group of friends and mentors for whom I feel so much gratitude, and many parts of me are sad that I can't possibly include everyone here.

Sometimes a single moment suddenly resonates with a profoundly liberating truth, and life changes. For me, one of those was reading Colin Wilson's advice to "live as if at any moment you can get the absurd good news." And the absurd good news keeps pouring in.

Gary Austin, the improvisational theater teacher who founded the Groundlings, helped me and all his lucky students everywhere, fly where hilarity, grief, and passion merge, granting permission to play with every self we have.

I bow in reverence to the innovator Brett Bevell — author, reiki master, and Omega Institute for Holistic Studies program strategist — who not only invited me to be a resident artist at Hermitage House tucked away on Omega's campus, where I worked on early drafts of this book, but also to teach voice dialogue and become part of Omega's esteemed faculty.

Synchronicity gets the credit for pointing me to voice dialogue and my mentors Hal and Sidra Stone. While I was seeking tools for enhancing creativity, I encountered their exhilarating embodied techniques of healing and transformation. Without them this book wouldn't exist. They also connected me to my passionate and incredibly knowledgeable editor, Georgia Hughes, and to the whole team of New World Library Publishing including Kristen Cashman, Tracy Cunningham, Tona Pearce Myers, Kim Corbin, Munro Magruder, and freelance editor Erika Büky. Thank you.

At my computer one evening in February 2019, I realized I had finished my book. I had nothing more to say. I'd crossed the finish line. Much to my surprise, it was an intense and quiet victory. After privately relishing the moment, I walked into our living room to tell my cherished husband, Ray. He literally dropped everything, including the TV remote control, and read the manuscript immediately. He and his daughter — my beloved Charlotte, an inspirational, multitalented, multimedia writer, performer, and shadow puppeteer — were the first people I'd ever met who defined themselves as lucky. They have always supported my creativity. I am so grateful for your love. Thank you.

I wish I had the space to list the specific and vital ways every member of my varying tribes has contributed to my life. Very simply, thank you all. Thank you, East Hill Riders from way back when; my longtime friends Jean Lucus DelPiano and the whole family, Jean and Meindert Anderson, Alma and Gina Henderson. Thank you, influential, diverse members of the revolutionary tribe I met when I met Ray, including Candy and Tej Hazarika, whose early Cool Grove Press encouragement I am grateful for; Ricki Roer, a constant role model for love, enjoyment, and excellence; Paul McIsaac, who introduced me to the wild worlds of experiential group work via an Amy and Arnold Mindell Process weekend; the legendary Ellen Meyers; Barbara Zeller, who one New Year's Eve launched another life transition for me when she told me it was possible to combine humor and healing (I was enrolled in Columbia University's School of Social Work within months); sister in the trenches Didi Rick and her husband, Barry Scheck; Wendy Keyes; Dan Scheffey; Sharon Burke; Kristen Lowman and Harris Yulin; Gail Pellett and Stephan VanDam; Steve Ditlea and Nancy Stedman; the Reinis family; J. P. Harpignes, whose influence includes recommending me to the Open Center and other psychedelic encounters; my Pacific Coast hosts, Adam Raskin and Adelina Arambula; every generation of the Shea family, who led me to my divine camaraderie with Peeka Trenkle, whose wisdom and inspiration traverse realms, including emboldening me to keep bees. Thank you to the lifelong friends I've encountered in my acting, improv, and writing tribes: Jeri Slater, with whom I've shared a wide variety of enriching experiences; Liz Quinn, with her influential and generous intelligence; Marlene Wallace and Thomas Hays, who singularly and together blow my mind with their extraordinary aesthetic and resilience; Mitzi Sinnott; Abra Bigham; Beth Stevens, who invigorates me with her restless intellect and singular affection; and Fran Sorin, who took my breath away when I met her and remains a source of connection, support, and ingenuity. Thank you to my vision quest tribe, including Reggie Marra, Jay Stearns, Lisa McCall, Jane Baniewicz, Michael Sallustio, Tracey Burke, Joanna Burgess, Christiane Munier,

Autumn Van Ord, and Barbara Bitondo, as well as Peter Lengsfelder, Amy Levek, Carolyn Lyday, Cathy Edgerly, Trebbe Johnson, Vanessa Vergnetti (whose strength in so many realms is an inspiration), Jeannie Gunter (who is a source of delight, magic, and evolution), and Mark Daley; and to my voice dialogue tribe — my two protégés Ruthie Fraser and Eric Potempa, Hannah Miller, Anne Desmond, Tamar Stone, Alice Simmonds, Mary Disharoon, Larry Novick, Martha-Lou Wolff, Catherine Keir, Marsha Sheldon, Abby Rosen, Susan Filley, Nancy Young, Pierre Cauvin, Genevieve Cailloux, Anna Ivara, John Swaner, Francesca Starr, the Dougherty family, John Cooper, Pam Winkler, Francine Pinto, Judith Hendin, Dorsey Cartwright and Neil Melli, Dulce Ivancko, Bonnie Bernell, Susanna Lerch and Urs Haeusermann, Dominick Schoenborn, Elaine Rosenson, Paolo Sacchetti, Scott Kellogg (whose pioneering spirit has awakened mine), and deep divers Dona Difler, Karen Thomas, Karen Olshansky, Linda Seeman, and Bonnie Pfeiffer (whose wisdom, warmth, and originality I prize). Thank you to my clinical tribe, including Debra Burrell and Barry Cohen, executive director of the Expressive Therapies Summit, who gave me a chance; and colleagues turned friends Alexandra Milonas, who galvanizes with her keen intellect and loyalty, and Reji Mathew, whose ferocious artistry, love, and strength are breathtaking and motivating. Thank you for contributing your many gifts, including your flair for narrative imagery to create my website from scratch and for always staunchly defending the concept of the final eighth!

Thank you to my large extended family, including my late father, Jake Dengel, and my mother, June Duffy, who taught me that nobody is too old to start anew; my talented sisters, Laura Catherine Brown, Alexis Dengel, and Julia Dengel; my brothers-in-law, Tony Brown and Anthony Braun; my nieces and nephew, Sarai, Ritter, and Myriah Dengel; my Gaspard sisters- and brothers-in-law Lorraine and Karl Armelin, Barbara Lawson, Diane Gaspard, Janet Gaspard, Elaine Gaspard, and Thom Branch, who were there in the penultimate leg of my writing, offering encouragement and delicious food at La Terre, in the south of France. Thanks to the wonderful Schulberg family, who have always supported my creativity. Thank you to my aunts, uncles, and cousins in the Duffy, Meyers, Refvem, and Taylor families. I know we will continue to laugh and cry together. I am grateful for the O'Connor family and especially for my beloved, innovative, and accomplished coseeker and author Brian O'Connor, and Josh Yu.

Thank you to Judith Stone for your early editing help, and to my talented photographer, Harry Pocius. I also want to thank a few people who dislodged some ridiculous perspectives I held and introduced me to new ones: Diane Austin, Barbara Biziou, John DaPolito, Caymichael Patten, Vanessa Brand, Valerie Larabee, Annette Lieberman, Jean Houston, Connie Buffalo, and Bill Gates of the Actors Fund.

I have eternal appreciation and gratitude for my brave clients and workshop participants, who trust me with their vulnerability and well-being. You inspire me and have made me who I am.

Notes

p. 6   *"Many researchers now believe"*: Paul Bloom, "First Person Plural," *Atlantic*, November 2008, www.theatlantic.com /magazine/archive/2008/11/first-person-plural/307055/.

p. 7   *"by toggling the way we address the self"*: Pamela Weintraub, "The Voice of Reason," *Psychology Today*, May 4, 2015, www .psychologytoday.com/articles/201505/the-voice-reason.

p. 10   *Self-care even makes you smarter*: Weintraub, "The Voice of Reason."

p. 25   *A Protector/Controller self is "like a bodyguard"*: Hal Stone and Sidra Stone, *Embracing Our Selves: The Voice Dialogue Manual* (Novato, CA: New World Library, 1989), 15.

p. 70   *there are physiological, psychological, and even evolutionary reasons*: Clifford Ivor Nass and Corina Yen, *The Man Who Lied to His Laptop: What Machines Teach Us about Human Relationships* (New York: Current, 2010).

p. 72   *"Like a well-trained CIA agent"*: Hal Stone and Sidra Stone, *Embracing Your Inner Critic: Turning Self-Criticism into a Creative Asset* (San Francisco: HarperSanFrancisco, 1993), 12.

p. 73   *the Inner Critic "has a great talent for teamwork"*: Stone and Stone, *Embracing Our Selves*, 114.

p. 73   *"at some point the Critic oversteps its bounds"*: Stone and Stone, *Embracing Your Inner Critic*, 12.

p. 85   *"it is important to go beyond the details of content"*: Stone and Stone, *Embracing Our Selves*, 121.

p. 85   *The sociologist Gregory Bateson defines the double bind*:

G. Bateson, D. D. Jackson, J. Haley, and J. Weakland, "Toward a Theory of Schizophrenia," *Behavioral Science* 1 (1956): 251–64.

p. 123   *Hal and Sidra Stone describe the Inner Critic as having "the intelligence of a genius"*: Stone and Stone, *Embracing Your Inner Critic*, chapter 1.

List of Exercises

Index

About the Author

Bridgit Dengel Gaspard is a writer, therapist, coach, and master facilitator and trainer of voice dialogue who has led professional workshops for the Omega Institute, the New York Open Center, the International Coach Federation, the Expressive Therapies Summit, Conscious Life Expo, New York University, Columbia University School of Social Work, the National Association of Social Workers, the Actors Fund, and other organizations. During her career in acting, improvisation, and comedy, she discovered voice dialogue, a powerful technique of communicating and embodying our inner selves developed by Drs. Hal and Sidra Stone, who would become her mentors.

She earned a master's degree in social work from Columbia University, acquiring clinical experience in dialectical behavior therapy (DBT) and cognitive behavioral therapy (CBT). She was an inpatient social worker at Bellevue Hospital Center and Creedmoor Psychiatric Center. She also worked as a psychotherapist at the New York University Counseling Center. She founded the New York Voice Dialogue Institute and has been certified by multiple organizations for continuing education credits for social workers, mental health practitioners, nurses, body workers, psychologists, psychiatrists, psychotherapists, massage therapists, and life coaches.

Bridgit maintains a private practice in Manhattan specializing in creativity blocks, life transitions, and being stuck in sight of the finish line. She lives in Brooklyn, New York.

www.final8th.com

NEW WORLD LIBRARY is dedicated to publishing books and other media that inspire and challenge us to improve the quality of our lives and the world.

We are a socially and environmentally aware company. We recognize that we have an ethical responsibility to our readers, our authors, our staff members, and our planet.

We serve our readers by creating the finest publications possible on personal growth, creativity, spirituality, wellness, and other areas of emerging importance. We serve our authors by working with them to produce and promote quality books that reach a wide audience. We serve New World Library employees with generous benefits, significant profit sharing, and constant encouragement to pursue their most expansive dreams.

Whenever possible, we print our books with soy-based ink on 100 percent postconsumer-waste recycled paper. We power our offices with solar energy and contribute to nonprofit organizations working to make the world a better place for us all.

Our products are available wherever books are sold. Visit our website to download our catalog, subscribe to our e-newsletter, read our blog, and link to authors' websites, videos, and podcasts.

customerservice@newworldlibrary.com
Phone: 415-884-2100 or 800-972-6657
Orders: Ext. 10 • Catalog requests: Ext. 10
Fax: 415-884-2199

www.newworldlibrary.com